The Making of Roman York

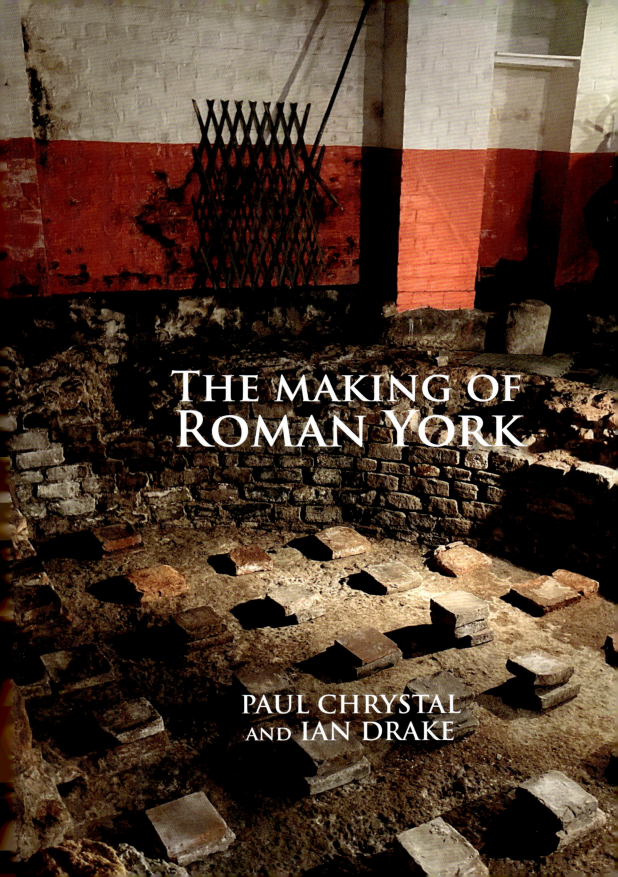

The making of Roman York

PAUL CHRYSTAL and IAN DRAKE

Paul Chrystal
Ian Drake, Council Member, YAYAS

Beware how you destroy your antiquities, guard them with religious care! They are what give you a decided character and superiority over other provincial cities. You have lost much, take care of what remains.

William Etty 1787–1849 on the precarious situation of York's antiquities then, as indeed they are now.

In the earliest records of English History, Ebor, Eboracum or York, is represented as a place of great importance; and, in the zenith of meridian splendour, it was the residence of Imperial Power, and the legislative seat of the Roman Empire. Hence we may readily suppose, especially when the ancient historic accounts of this city are contrasted with those of London, that York far exceeded in dignity and consequence, if not in population and extent, the present capital of the British Empire, at that period.

William Hargrove, History of York, 1818.

First published in 2022
by Palatine Books,
Carnegie House,
Chatsworth Road
Lancaster LA1 4SL
www.palatinebooks.com

Copyright © Paul Chrystal and Ian Drake

All rights reserved
Unauthorised duplication contravenes existing laws

The right of Paul Chrystal and Ian Drake to be identified as the authors of this work has been asserted in accordance with the Copyright, Designs and Patents act 1988

British Library Cataloguing-in-Publication data
A catalogue record for this book is available from the British Library

Every effort has been made to trace copyright holders. Some of the images used in this publication are orphaned images from the collections at Lancaster City Museums. If you are the creator or rights holder of any of these images, please do get in touch.

Paperback ISBN 13: 978-1-910837-31-3

Designed and typeset by Carnegie Book Production
www.carnegiebookproduction.com

Printed and bound by Cambrian

Halftitle page image: The Legio IX inscription: a superb fortress inscription from one of the main gates of the Roman fortress and one of the best examples of epigraphy to emerge from Roman Britain (*RIB* 665)

Title page images: (left) The Multangular Tower interior. The tower stands just over 9 metres tall in total. The lower 6 metres were built by the Romans. A square stone called the 'saxa quadrata' makes up the internal and external skin, a layer of red tiles then acts as a modern day wall-tie does, holding the two layers together and creating a solid structure, one which has certainly stood the test of time; (right) Roman Bath Museum – The amazingly well preserved hypocaust in the museum in 2022

About the Authors

Paul Chrystal has classics degrees from the Universities of Hull and Southampton. After that he went into medical publishing for forty or so years but now combines this with writing features for national and local newspapers and history magazines such as *Minerva Magazine, BBC History, Ancient History, All About History, Omnibus* and *Ad Familiares*. He appears regularly on BBC local radio, on the BBC World Service and Radio 4's PM programme. He has been history advisor for a number of York tourist attractions and is the author of over 130 books on a wide range of subjects, including many on York and ancient history. One of his latest books is *The Romans in the North of England* (2019).

He is a regular reviewer for and contributor to *Classics for All*, and a contributor to the classics section of the Oxford University Press *Oxford Bibliographies Online*. He writes endorsements for Yale University Press in London and New York. In 2019, Paul was guest speaker for the prestigious Vassar College New York's London Programme in association with Goldsmith University. Paul lives just outside York.

Ian Drake attended Archbishop Holgate's Grammar School and has been in the York area for over 50 years. He is Keeper of the Evelyn Collection for the Yorkshire Architectural and York Archaeological Society and is an active member of the Association of Voluntary Guides for the City of York and York Archaeological Trust. He is the Honorary Treasurer and Trustee for the Council of British Archaeology Yorkshire. He regularly gives talks to many organisations in the area on a series of York related topics. He is co-author with Paul Chrystal of two new books on York: *Life in York 100 Years Ago* which showcases rarely seen photographs from the unique Thomas Hancock collection held by YAYAS; and *York: A Rare Insight* – exclusive photographs from the Evelyn Collection.

*In memory of Timothy Thomas Bennett Ryder 1930–2021,
my tutor at Hull University 1973–1976*

Acknowledgements

Thanks are due to a number of people and associations who have helped us make this book a lot better than it would have been without their generous interventions. They are, in no particular order: Martin Drake for redrawing the map of the Roman York walk; Kurt Hunter-Mann BA (Hons), MCIfA, Research Associate, YAYAS and York Archaeological Trust for casting his expert eye over the archaeological bits and putting them right where necessary; Graham Harris for the Roman Bath Museum pictures; York Archaeological Trust for the photo taken at their Tang Hall DIG event and for those relating to the 'Headless gladiators' excavations – and for many others: especially Sarah Maltby, Adam Raw-Mackenzie and last but certainly not least Louis Carter and Aislinn Dowling (DIG) for all the hard work and sterling service they provided. Richard Saward, Head of Visitor Experience and Commercial; and Andrew Woods, Senior Curator (Yorkshire Museum) at the Yorkshire Museum in York, as well as Rebecca Vickers who painstakingly sourced all the museum photos for us; Geoff Cook, Rheolwr Cynadleddau a Digwyddiadau – Conference & Events Manager, Neuadd Y Ddinas –City Hall, Caerdydd – Cardiff for the image of the wonderful statue of Boudica. Professor Tod Bolen at Bibleplaces.com, Santa Clarita, CA for the photo of the Masada siege tower. The frightening image of Arminius comes courtesy of Digital Park, Lage, Germany. The vivid and dramatic Legio VI pictures at the 2019 York Roman Festival come courtesy of Legio VI Victrix – Dave aka Marcus and Charlotte Graham Photography. Thanks too to Simone Dunn, Front of House Manager at York Theatre Royal, for the picture of the Roman well and to Ben Pilgrim, Royal Pilgrim Communications, for the conjectural images of the Roman Quarter. Jay Commins at York Archaeology has kindly provided images and information relating to the proposed York Quarter and the forthcoming (summer 2022) radar survey of 20km of York streets searching for Roman remains.

As always we have tried our hardest to obtain permission for anything which is or may be copyright; if anything has slipped through the net please accept our apologies and do advise us so that we can ensure that due credit is given in any reprint or new edition.

Roman Inscriptions in Britain (*RIB*)

Throughout the book we have used *RIB* numbers to identify Roman inscriptions in the text. According to the website (romaninscriptionsofbritain.org) '*RIB* online … hosts Volume One of *The Roman Inscriptions of Britain*, R.G. Collingwood's and R.P. Wright's magisterial edition of 2,401 monumental inscriptions from Britain found prior to 1955. It also incorporates all Addenda and Corrigenda published in the 1995 reprint of *RIB* (edited by R.S.O. Tomlin) and the annual survey of inscriptions published in Britannia since … *RIB* Online endeavours to faithfully reproduce the printed edition and the relevant addenda and corrigenda published in *Journal of Roman Studies and Britannia*'.

In book form *Roman Inscriptions of Britain* is a 3-volume corpus of inscriptions found in Britain from the Roman period – an encyclopedic work initiated by Francis J. Haverfield – whose notebooks were bequeathed to the University of Oxford. The first volume, *Inscriptions on Stone* was then edited by R. G. Collingwood and R. P. Wright with an addendum by R. S. O. Tomlin. It was first published in 1965, with a new edition in 1995. Volume II mainly covers the inscriptions found on domestic utensils. Volume III (edited by R. S. O. Tomlin, R. P. Wright, and M. W. C. Hassall) is a continuation of Volume I, containing all the lapidary inscriptions found from the closing date of volume I to 31 December 2006. The *Corpus Inscriptionum Latinarum* (CIL) is a comprehensive collection of ancient Latin inscriptions forming an equally authoritative source for documenting the surviving epigraphy of classical antiquity. Public and personal inscriptions throw light on all aspects of Roman life and history. The *Corpus* continues to be updated in new editions and supplements.

Contents

About the authors	v
Acknowledgements	vii
Roman Inscriptions in Britain	viii
Preface	xi
PART ONE: A walk around Roman York and what you can see	1
PART TWO: Introduction: Roman Britain AD 71–AD 410	29
Recent excavations and what we learn from them: 1970–2020	41
Fortress York: from wooden fort to *colonia*	56
A life in the day of a Roman in York I	61
The early occupation and the fortress	65
The strategic importance of York: roads and rivers	77
The Garrison	82
The civilian settlement (*vicus* or *canaba*)	87
Burials and the headless gladiators	92
Trade and industry	109
The Romans are in the Undercroft	115
The Yorkshire Museum	120
The Roman Bath Museum	160
DIG York	162
Eboracum annual Roman Festival	164
A life in the day of a Roman in York II	166
Hoards found in York	169
Roman York in the future	176
Roman York timeline	180
Appendix 1: Select list of Roman emperors	185
Appendix 2: Governors of Britannia AD 43–97	188
Appendix 3: York's Medieval Churches built using Roman masonry	189
Appendix 4: Roman legions serving in Britannia	192
Some Latin terms	193
Further reading	197
Websites	207
Index	209
Index of places	211

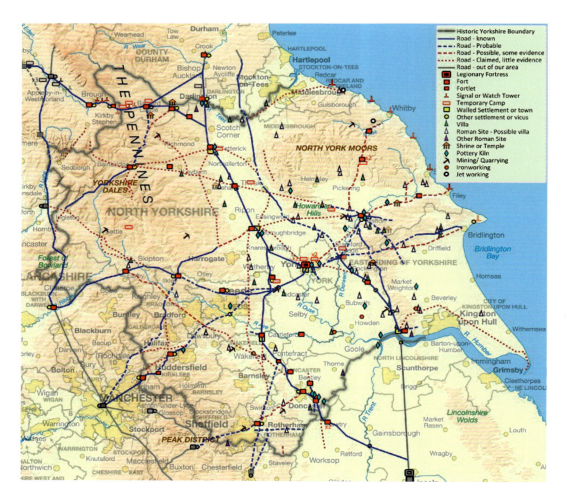

Roman Yorkshire

Preface

Astonishingly, given that York is first and foremost a Roman city, and was always an extremely important one at that, there are precious few recent books on the Roman presence in York available to the tens of thousands of visitors who flock to the city every year. One of the earlier publications which catered for this prodigious, seemingly unquenchable, demand was also called *Roman York* (1971), subtitled *A Pictorial Guide*; it was written by the late Herman Ramm and was published under the auspices of Yorkshire Architectural & York Archaeological Society. The book is long out of print and was of its time, but it did go into a respectable six editions in its 20 year life and provides the inspiration for our twenty-first-century pictorial guide to *Roman York*. Roman York itself has yielded much in the intervening years, all of which is recounted here.

This new *Roman York* is a comprehensive guide to the footprint left by the Romans in the city of York. It is fully illustrated and comes with clear maps to guide the visitor effortlessly around the sites and sights. Importantly, the book is written in a lively and engaging style which is accessible to the general reader, be they looking for a comprehensive tour of Roman York or just a selective outing.

To give a relatively accurate picture of what daily life must have been like in a place like Eboracum, to give it its Roman name, there are two 'Life in a day' chapters: one describes a day at the baths by a Roman jurist who actually lived in Roman York; the other is a letter by his brother serving with Agricola at the Battle of Mons Graupius.

Eboracum, like Rome, its mother city, was not built in a day. Nothing like it: the history of Roman York entails the unravelling of multiple layers of new development, refurbishment, military destruction, demolition and overbuilding over some 350 years. This unravelling is essentially what the book, and York, is all about. New finds are being uncovered all the time here; the book brings you right up to date with the very latest excavations from the fortress and the extensive surrounding civilian settlement, the *canabae* and the *vicus*; these include

- THE RYEDALE ROMAN HOARD. The three bronzes and plumb bob in the hoard date from the later 2nd century AD and offer a rare insight into a religious ceremony in rural Roman Yorkshire which culminated in the burial of these objects as an offering to the gods. On display in the Yorkshire Museum.
- 3 and 6 Driffield Terrace, 2004–5: 'gladiator' cemetery: 'The headless gladiators of York' as featured on TV
- St Leonard's Hospital 2001–4
- fortress SW defences (stone phase now dated to early second century)
- Hungate *c.*2006–12
- East Heslington (University of York), late 2000s
- Newington Hotel 2017–18 cemetery adjacent to the Trentholme Drive site

Other major discoveries in the last forty or so years include:

- GROUND PENETRATING RADAR under the streets of York to 'expose' as much of Eboracum as possible. Starts summer 2022.
- Blake Street – barrack buildings inside the fortress.
- Rougier Street – a building probably a warehouse in the *colonia*.
- Wellington Row – second-century stone building whose use is uncertain.
- Tanner Row – second-century timber building and stone building, late third century.
- Wellington Row – Tanner Row – road surface leading to possible site of Roman bridge over the river Ouse.
- Junction of Micklegate and Skeldergate – a substantial baths building.
- Inside the city walls under site of old railway station – further evidence of baths.

However, we start with a walk around the visible sights of Roman York – a walk which will educate and fascinate in equal measure, revealing as it does that footprint left by the Romans in Eboracum.

PART ONE
A WALK AROUND ROMAN YORK AND WHAT YOU CAN SEE

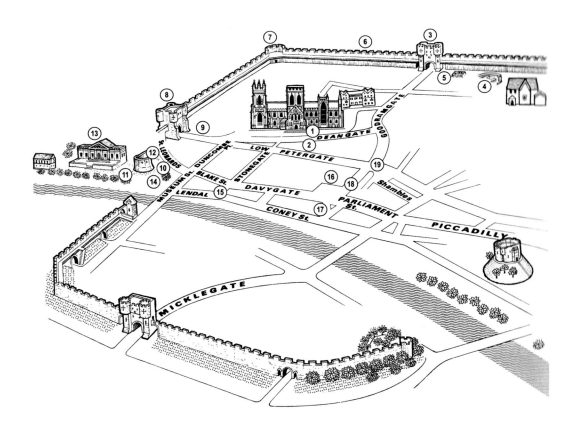

The route of the walk and the sights and sites to be seen on the walk

This easy walk follows a route around the principal sites of Roman York which are readily accessible and visible to visitors to the city and to residents. The walk concentrates on the north-east bank of the River Ouse, covering the fortress of Eboracum and its neighbouring *canaba*. There was a large civilian settlement (the *vicus*) on the south-west bank of the river which was awarded prestigious *colonia* status in AD 213. There is nothing of the south-west *colonia* visible although the known sites of some features are marked by information plaques or boards. While many of the sites have information boards of various types, this guide gives more detailed information on all of the sites.

The walk takes in three special locations which are home to some of the best collections of Roman artefacts in Britain – a reflection of the importance of Eboracum within the Roman Empire. These sites are The Yorkshire Museum, York Minster Undercroft Museum and The Roman Bath Museum.

Part of our route takes you onto York's medieval city walls which are open every day from dawn until dusk. The route should take the average person between one and one and a half hours, not including any visits to the museums.

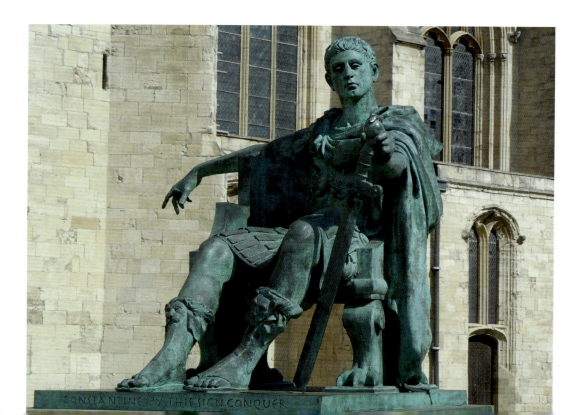

#1 The walk starts outside the south door of York Minster at the statue of emperor Constantine the Great sitting regally, surveying his fortress. There is a descriptive plaque next to the statue which reads …'

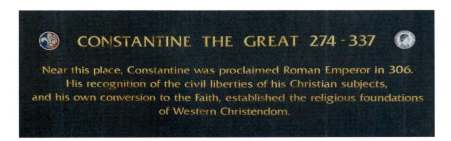

The sculptor, Philip Jackson, was fastidious in his research on the clothing, seating and armour of the period. The result is a 'fascinating medley of fact and conjecture'. The emperor gazes down at his broken sword, which forms the shape of a cross, a moving emblem of Constantine's world-changing act of making Christianity a legal and (largely) tolerated religion of the hitherto predominantly pagan Roman Empire.

The Undercroft Museum is accessible from inside the minster, featuring structural remains of the Roman fortress headquarters (*principium*) and parts of the First Cohort centurions' quarters, along with one of the sewers serving the fortress. Entrance to the Undercroft Museum is through the west end of the Minster. Remains of the Roman basilica building, at the north side of the *principia,* are visible in the undercroft.

Excavated wall and drain under the Minster

While you are in the Minster, take time to see St Stephen's Chapel at the north-east corner beyond the choir. Its terracotta panel is called 'The First Hour of the Crucifixion' and was created by the ceramic artist George Tinworth. The relief shows early afternoon on Good Friday when the other two of the three crosses are being erected. Roman soldiers are casting lots as to who should get Christ's robes after his crucifixion and the same soldiers are shown dividing up his clothes. Note the Victorian moustaches sported by the soldiers and the little boy on the right who seems to be enjoying the Eucharist wine.

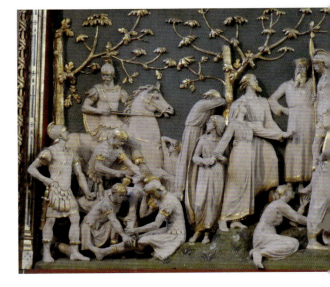

#2 Once outside again, head towards the 25 ft column which formed part of the *principia*, discovered when the Minster's central tower was underpinned in the 1960s.

The plaque on the column reads:

THIS ROMAN COLUMN ONCE STOOD WITHIN THE GREAT HALL OF THE HEADQUARTERS BUILDING OF THE FORTRESS OF THE SIXTH LEGION (WHOSE EMBLEM WAS A BULL) IN THE FOURTH CENTURY A.D. IT WAS FOUND IN 1969 DURING THE EXCAVATION OF THE SOUTH TRANSEPT OF THE MINSTER, LYING WHERE IT HAD COLLAPSED. IT WAS GIVEN BY THE DEAN AND CHAPTER TO THE YORK CIVIC TRUST WHO IN 1971 ERECTED IT ON THIS SITE TO MARK THE 1900TH ANNIVERSARY OF THE FOUNDATION OF THE CITY BY THE ROMANS IN A.D. 71.

The column in 2019 and when it was found in 1968

#3 Follow the path around the east end of the Minster past the Stonemason's Yard and turn right past the half-timbered building, St William's College in College Street, and then left into Goodramgate. Monk Bar is in front of you at the end.

#4 Go up onto the wall by the steps, turning right at the top and walk for about 40 metres. Below you will see the rounded remains of the east corner tower known as the Aldwark Tower, and an interval tower.

#5 At this corner the fortress wall stands to its full height, excluding the parapet, of 5 metres. Explanation boards are attached to the city walls railings.

Although it is no longer accessible, this corner has a building inscription of the Xth Cohort (*RIB* 668) found in 1946. It is built into the outer face of the Roman fortress-wall 2 metres above the chamfered footing nearly in the centre of the rectangular turret. Return to Monk Bar, go back down to street level, cross the road and go up on to the walls by the steps in Monk Bar. Turn left, as you head towards Bootham Bar you are walking on the thirteenth-century wall built on top of a series of earlier mounds which overlie the Roman fortress wall.

#6 Pause when you reach a round plaque set into the walkway pavement. You are now near the site of one of the four gates into the fortress – the *porta decumana*, although there are no Roman remains visible.

#7 Continue along the walls past Gray's Court and the Deanery on your left. The walls eventually take a 90 degree turn to the left – you are now actually following the precise line of the Roman fortress. This is what is known as Robin Hood Tower, although there is no connection with the folk hero. From here you can look back to your right along the course of the medieval moat, outside the walls and further out than the earlier Roman ditch. The angle marks the north corner of the fortress.

#8 The view inside this stretch of wall is one of the finest in York, taking in the Minster, the Chapter House and the Minster Library (the old archbishop's palace); continue to Bootham Bar.

#9 Look down through the arrow slits to the left inside the Bar to see the street below, High Petergate, part of the *via principalis* of the fortress.

THE ROMAN WALLS

lettering based on medieval masons' marks

In AD 71, the Roman army established a fortress on the banks of the River Ouse called *Eboracum*. You are standing above the remains of the eastern corner tower of this fortress and, further to your right, those of an interval tower. The fortress was rectangular in shape and covered an area of 20 hectares (50 acres). There were four large gatehouses on the sites of today's St Helen's Square, King's Square, north-east of the Treasurer's House and under Bootham Bar. The wall here stands to its original height of 5 metres and the tower rose at least 3 metres above that. The wall continues beneath the grass, as present ground level is nearly 3 metres higher than that of the Roman city.

The Romans left York around AD 410 but the legacy of their defensive walls remains. In generally good condition the north-west and north-east walls still stand today. They are only visible in a few places as they are covered by the grassed-over medieval ramparts. Excavations in York have revealed clues to life in the fortress, including barrack blocks, bathhouses and an elaborate system of drains and sewers, but much still remains hidden beneath our feet.

A coin bearing the profile of the Emperor Septimius Severus. The Imperial Roman Court was based in York for three years during the war against the rebellious northern tribes. Severus, born in Africa, died in York in AD 211.

Come down from the walls at Bootham Bar. At the bottom of the steps there are information plaques. Bootham Bar overlies another gateway in the fortress – the *porta principalis dextra* – part of which is preserved in the floor of the modern building (a café) adjoining the Bar.

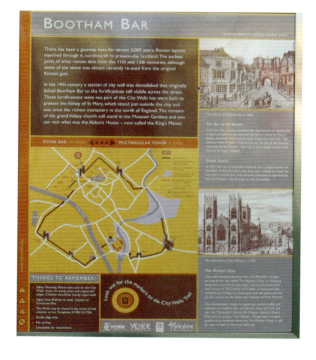

A WALK AROUND ROMAN YORK AND WHAT YOU CAN SEE

Turn left and on your left in the coffee house (Bean & Gone) you can see the lower courses of the fortress wall immediately next to the *porta principalis dextra* (ie the main gate on the right side) through a glass panel in the floor. This is a fragment of the foundations of the western curtain wall. The remains were first revealed and recorded in 1910 during building works on the site, but the wall was then concealed in a shallow basement for more than 100 years.

#10 Retrace your steps and cross the road towards the William Etty statue and fountain in front of the City Art Gallery. Turn left towards the white Georgian terrace. On the grassed area between the pavement and the car park you can see another small section of the fortress wall. A plaque records that it was built under the emperor Constantius Chlorus in about AD 300.

Across the road, under the stage in the Theatre Royal, there are the remains of a Roman well. Unfortunately, but for obvious reasons, you can only see this on one of the organised tours of the theatre.

The well; courtesy and © York Theatre Royal

#11 Go back towards the City Art Gallery and turn sharp left down the lane between two stone walls with King's Manor on your right. Pass through the gate into the Museum Gardens where you will see, to the left, the outside of the magnificent Multangular Tower – the west corner of the Roman fortress. One of its stone walls is twenty-one feet by eleven feet wide, and bears the legible inscription 'Genio loci feliciter': 'good luck to the guardian spirit of this place' – (Roman Inscriptions in Britain [RIB], 647). It was uncovered in 1702 when digging a cellar below the Black Swan Inn in Coney Street outside the south angle of the fortress and is now in the Yorkshire Museum (YORYM: 2007.6197).

Rebuilding of the defences in the third and fourth centuries is now doubted. The Multangular Tower is now thought to date to the early second century, and this dating probably applies to the entire south-west stone defences.

You have now walked exactly half way round the fortress. Adjoining the tower is a 46-foot section of the front fortress wall. This wall, over 16 feet high, stands to its full height (only the parapet is missing) and, with the Multangular Tower, ranks as one of the finest surviving pieces of Roman masonry in Britain.

The Multangular Tower is a multi-period structure; the lower 20 feet are Roman. What greater symbol of Rome's power?

The wall has no distinct plinth at its base and the rear face has been roughly finished; the reason for this is that it would have been largely obscured by the earthen rampart. At a height of over 7 feet, the facing stones are interrupted by a band of five red tile courses; there was a cornice of tiles at the top of the wall.

An early impression of the Quadrangular Tower from 1807

Retrace your steps for about 5 metres, follow the small path on your right passing through the medieval wall by a small door leading into the garden of the York City Library.

This gives you a view of the inside of the Multangular Tower and the fortress wall on either side of it. The interior of the front fortress wall to the left of the tower has lost its facing stones but that distinctive Roman band of red tiles can clearly be seen here.

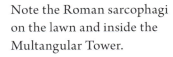

Note the Roman sarcophagi on the lawn and inside the Multangular Tower.

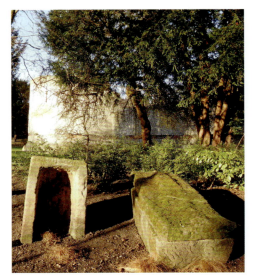

A WALK AROUND ROMAN YORK AND WHAT YOU CAN SEE

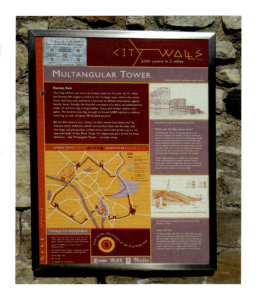

#12 There is an information board at the side of the small doorway. Take the path to your right between the fortress wall and the rear of the library, and go down the steps to see what is called the Anglian Tower.

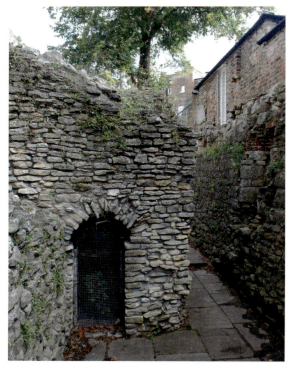

Beyond the Anglian Tower the reconstructed banks of the various heights of the city's ramparts from Roman times to the present day are visible.

Retrace your steps through the small doorway and turn left, back into the Museum Gardens.

#13 If you wish to visit the Yorkshire Museum, now is the time. The museum houses a large and accessible collection of Roman artefacts mostly from York and the surrounding area

Mars, god of war, greets you at the door. Photo courtesy of and © York Museums Trust.

#14 To continue your walk, head back past the Multangular Tower towards the main gate from the Museum Gardens. Just before the gate take the path on your left left towards the Norman archway; this is part of the remains of the medieval hospital of St Leonard built into the western corner of the Roman fortress. Inside the archway there is a series of information panels, the first of which details the Roman period activity in this area.

As you return to the exit look to your right to see the remains of a small section of the foundations of one of the six interval towers built along the front fortress wall.

The Ninth Legion built a massive fortress here when the Romans arrived in AD 71. Eboracum (York) was used as a base from which to control the North.

Originally it was a wooden structure, rebuilt in stone about AD 107. Towers that projected out from the walls were added in a later rebuilding phase; possibly for defence or for show. Part of the wall still remains near the main entrance and if you look closely you can see stones which protrude out from the line of the wall. This would have been one of the interval towers.

Although the fort was constructed nearly two thousand years ago, the West corner of it still towers above today's visitors. Known as the Multangular Tower, because of its many sides, the smaller stones laid by the Romans remain. The larger stones on the upper half of the tower are later medieval additions.

Artefacts from Roman York can be seen in the Yorkshire Museum. Stone sarcophagi from excavations of Roman burials can be found in the Gardens.

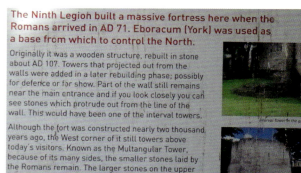

18   A WALK AROUND ROMAN YORK AND WHAT YOU CAN SEE

#15 Exit the gardens. Cross the road and walk down the left-hand side of Lendal in front of you. Go down a passage on the left. The cobbles set in the floor of the passage indicate the site of another of the interval towers of the fortress, the foundations of which were discovered in the 1970s. Returning to Lendal turn left: the fine Georgian town house on your left is the Judges' Lodgings built on the site of another late Roman interval tower; it was constructed in 1726 for a Dr Wintringham (d. 1748), a physician at York County Hospital from 1746. An effigy of Aesculapius, Roman god of medicine, appropriately guards the door.

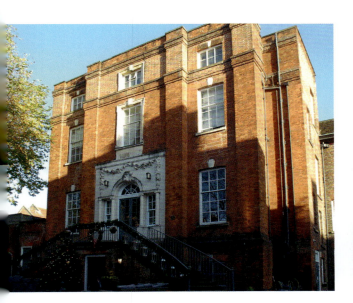

Now head down to the end of Lendal and go into St Helen's Square. Mansion House is on your right. This is the site of the south-west gate. There is a plaque on the wall of the former Yorkshire Insurance Building also on your right before Mansion House; the line of the front fortress wall is marked out in the paving across the Square.

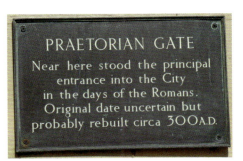

A WALK AROUND ROMAN YORK AND WHAT YOU CAN SEE

#16 Leave the square by the street to the right of St Helen's Church which is facing you; this is Davygate. In approximately 200 metres you will reach St Sampson's Square. The Roman Bath pub is to your left.

A slave market is said to have existed in St Sampson's Square during the Roman occupation. Later, Bede tells us that Pope Gregory I (d. 604) admired English slaves, punning *'non Angli sed angeli'* – 'they're not Angles, but angels'.

If you want to visit the Roman Bath Museum, go in through the door to the right and down the steps. The museum displays remains of part of the *caldarium* and hypocaust system excavated in 1930–1; this circulated hot air below the floor which was raised on pillars (*pilae*), warming up anyone relaxing in the *caldarium*. There are lots of descriptive displays illuminating all things Roman and visitors are free to dress up in items from a superb collection of reproduction Roman clothing and military uniforms.

A Roman tile (top) displaying the imprint of hobnail boots made by a Roman who walked on the wet clay tile, presumably left out in the sun to dry

Part of the hypocaust system, clearly showing the *pilae* (middle)

Reproduction military equipment and civilian clothing

Reproduction helmets and a *cornu* or *cornum*, an army signalling horn: it was a large G-shaped curved horn brass instrument about 3 metres (9.8 ft) long. The instrument was braced by a crossbar that gave rigidity to the structure and provided a means of supporting its weight on the player's shoulder. Two have been found in Pompeii. It was used by the army for communicating orders to troops in battle. In Roman art, the *cornu* often appears among the instruments that accompany games (*ludi*) or gladiator fights as on the Zliten mosaic (lower).

Blowing the *cornu*. A cornicen photographed by the photographer during a re-enactment of Legio XV from Pram, Austria. The *cornu* was carried by the *cornicen* (horn-blower) who 'translated' his commander's orders into signals and broadcast them over the field during battles. This file is licensed under the Creative Commons Attribution-Share Alike 3.0 Unported license

#17 From the Bath Museum go across St Sampson Square on to Parliament Street and go down Feasegate which is on your right. The junction of Feasegate and Market Street is the site (not visible) of the south tower of the fortress which is constructed to roughly the same plan as the Multangular Tower.

Turn right down Market Street, at the end turn left into Spurriergate and go the end to reach the corner of High Ousegate and Nessgate. Here the foundation stone on the wall of a bank on the corner of High Ousegate and Nessgate (*RIB* 648) is a copy of an important inscribed stone found (with *RIB* 656 and 698) when the building was being built in 1839. The original is in the Yorkshire Museum (YORYM: 2007.6186). It describes the restoration of a temple dedicated to Hercules. References to the Roman name for York, Eboracum, are very rare and this is the only record of it to have been found. It translates as 'To Hercules ... Titus Perpetuius (?) Aetern[us] ... of the colony of York ... restored ...'. The size of the stone would suggest that at least half is missing. The names in ll. 2 and 3 belong to more than one man.

#18 Retrace your steps to St Sampson's Square and go towards St Sampson's church on your right, in Church Street. Under here lies a 52-metre length of the main sewer serving the Roman baths. It is only accessible on special open days. In 1972 the sewer was discovered on the north side of Church Street where waste water from the baths and latrines would have been washed away. It extended for 44 metres and was high enough to allow slaves to crawl along inside to clean it. Side channels, sluices and manhole covers are also in evidence. Analysed sewerage shows the residents of York to have been riddled with worms and bowel parasites. The discovery of spicules from marine sponges confirms what we already knew from literary evidence: that bathers used sponges as 'toilet paper' – probably for communal and not individual, personal use.

#19 Continue along Church Street to King's Square on your right – the site of the *'porta principalis sinistra'* – literally translated as 'the gate at the left-hand end of the transverse street'. King's Square is at the junction of Petergate, Goodramgate and Church Street.

A number of York's medieval churches were built using stone from Roman buildings. They are described in the Epilogue.

Photo Arthur MacGregor

This brings you to the end of the walk. The following may also be of interest:

Treasurer's House

Behind the Chapter House at the Minster. A Roman street, the *Via Decumana*, was excavated here under the cellar of the house in the 1960s, lending credence to stories about ghostly legionaries marching through.

Stonegate

Stonegate refers to the road leading to and from the Roman *Porta Praetoria*, a gate into the Roman garrison. The old Roman stone paving – which gives us the modern name – survives under the cobbles complete with the central gulley for the chariots' skid wheels.

Plaques celebrating Roman York are at Bootham Bar; Praetorian Gate, St Helen's Square; the Roman Column; Stonegate; Petergate; Constantine

the Great statue; Roman Wall in St Leonard's Place, the Anglian Tower in Library Gardens.

The numbers on the walk

1. Constantine statue, York Minster with Undercroft Museum and St Stephen's Chapel
2. Roman Column
3. Monk Bar
4. Aldwark Tower
5. Interval tower
6. Plaque in floor
7. Robin Hood Tower
8. Bootham Bar
9. Petergate
10. Wall in St Leonard's
11. Multangular Tower
12. Anglian Tower
13. Yorkshire Museum
14. St Leonard's Arch
15. St Helen's Square
16. Roman Bath Museum
17. Market St./Feasegate
18. Church Street
19. King's Square

Streets (*viae*) and gates (*portae*) in Eboracum

Via principalis, main street – Petergate

Via praetoria, Stonegate. The street leading from the front of the headquarters building to the front gate.

Via decumana, Chapter House Street. The road linking the gates in the long sides and passing in front of the *principia*.

Porta principalis dextra – under Bootham Bar. The gate at the right-hand end of the main transverse street.

Porta principalis sinistra – under King's Square. The gate at the left-hand end of the transverse street.

Porta praetoria – under St Helen's Square

Porta decumana – in the garden at Gray's Court

The second part of the book details many of the features of the city which made York what it was in the the Roman period, how it functioned and the people who live there.

Roman Britain in the first century AD

PART TWO

Introduction: Roman Britain AD 71–AD 410: 'A place of some importance'

York (Eboracum) is founded; the Agricola campaigns

York was founded in AD 71 as Eboracum, later capital of Northern Britain, a *colonia* and always a fortress. It was founded not as a result of considered strategic planning but as the response to an emergency and a need to monitor and contain the troublesome and hostile activity of the Parisi and the Brigantes. York was a military epicentre within and an entrepôt for northern Roman Britain. It was a launching point for punitive raids as required to the north, east, west and south. It was a huge supply depot for military activity all round and the far north; it was a command centre for all military operations in the north of England. Settlements were erected on the higher, better-drained land on the Wolds and the fringes of Holderness, the Vale of Pickering and the central Vales of Mowbray and York.

Quintus Petillius Cerialis defeated Venutius, the king of the Brigantes, near Stanwick around 70. In 71, as Tacitus says, he continued his successful campaign against the Brigantes whose territory extended to the Solway-Tyne line. Tacitus praised both Cerialis and his successor Julius Frontinus (governor 75–78) for a job well done.

These successes led to the assimilation into the empire of the soon-to-be-Romanised Brigantes and Parisi tribes. Frontinus had been sent into Britannia in 74 to succeed Quintus Petillius Cerialis as governor. He finally subdued the Silures and other hostile Welsh tribes, establishing a new base at Caerleon for Legio II Augusta (Isca Augusta) and a network of smaller forts fifteen to twenty kilometres apart for his auxiliary units. He also may have established the fort at Pumsaint in west Wales, to exploit the gold deposits at Dolaucothi. He retired in 78, and later was appointed water commissioner in Rome. The new governor was Gnaeus Julius Agricola, Tacitus' father-in-law.

For the Romans, the long-term effect of Boudica's revolt in AD 60/61 had quite obviously been to increase their resolve to subdue and Romanise Britannia – a feat which was more or less accomplished, for a time, under Agricola.

There were undoubted economic benefits in exploiting the raw materials of this northern region but the prime motive for occupation was always military. The belligerent Picts and Scots were kept down by stationing Legio IX in the area; consequently, the majority of the Roman settlements north of the Humber were military stations. The Romans built military facilities in the Pennines at Ilkley, Castleshaw and Slack, to monitor and control the Brigantes, and temporary Roman military camps on the North York Moors at Cawthorne and Goathland. There were, however, signs of non-military civilisation with Roman villas around Derventio (Malton), Petuaria (Brough on Humber) and in the area around present-day Bridlington. A line of signal stations, one of which is located at Castle Hill, Scarborough, was built along the North Yorkshire coast from Saltburn in the north to warn of the approach of shipping, hostile or otherwise.

Tacitus' *Agricola* 21 gives us something of a template for the process of Romanisation as deployed throughout the Empire, although it must be viewed in the light of the undeniable fact that Tacitus was keen to 'big up' his father-in-law, and that he, cynically, saw through the process as just another form of servitude in which the locals had turned soft:

> The following winter passed without trouble, and was spent in salutary measures. For, in order to get a population which

was scattered and barbarous and therefore inclined to war, accustomed to rest and repose through the seduction of luxury, Agricola gave private encouragement and public finance to the building of temples, courts of justice and housing, praising the industrious, and rebuking the indolent. Thus an honourable rivalry took the place of compulsion. He likewise provided a liberal education for the sons of the chiefs, and showed a preference for the natural powers of the Britons over the good worth ethic of the Gauls that they who lately scorned Latin now craved its eloquence. Hence, too, a liking sprang up for our style of dress, and the *toga* became all the rage. Step by step they were led to things which dispose to vice, laziness, the bath, the elegant banquet. In their ignorance they called all this 'civilization', when it was just part of their servitude.

Agricola started as he meant to go on, first dealing severely with the Ordovices of north Wales, who had destroyed a cavalry wing of Roman auxiliaries stationed on their land. Agricola had served in Britannia before and used this experience to move quickly to defeat and virtually annihilate the rebels. He then invaded Anglesey, home to the terror-inspiring druids and forced a peace. Next he attacked the Brigantes and the Selgovae on the southern coast of Scotland, using his overwhelming war machine to re-establish Roman control.

In 80, Agricola marched to the Firth of Tay (some historians hold that he stopped along the Firth of Forth in that year), not returning south until 81, at which time he consolidated his gains in the new territory he had conquered, and in the rebellious lands that he had re-conquered. In 82 he sailed to either Kintyre or the shores of Argyll, or to both. In 83 and 84 he moved north along Scotland's eastern and northern coasts, deploying both land and naval forces, campaigning successfully against the inhabitants, and winning a significant victory over the northern British peoples led by Calgacus at the decisive Battle of Mons Graupius.

Prior to his recall in 84, Agricola built a network of military roads and forts to secure the Roman occupation. Existing forts were strengthened, and new ones constructed in the north east of Scotland along the Highland Line, consolidating control of the glens that provided access to and from the Scottish Highlands. The line of military communication and supply along south-eastern Scotland and north-eastern England (i.e. Dere Street) was amply fortified. In southern-most Caledonia, the lands of the Selgovae (approximating to modern Dumfriesshire and the Stewartry of Kirkcudbright) were heavily planted with forts, not only establishing effective control there, but also completing a military enclosure of south-central Scotland.

Hadrian's Wall and the Antonine Wall

But the Romans had patently over-extended themselves; not for the last time did wider security issues in the greater empire dictate policy in Britannia. Agricola was recalled to Rome by Domitian (AD 81–AD 96).

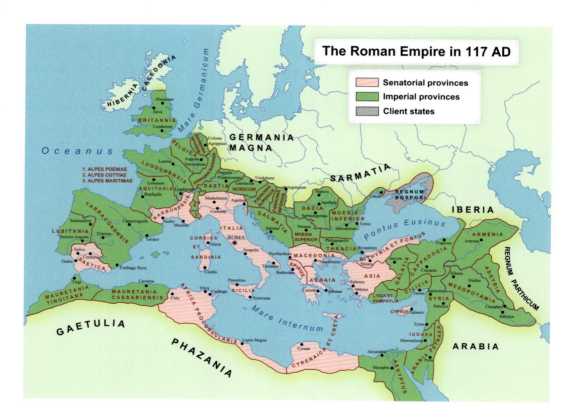

In 2010, to commemorate the 1600th anniversary of the end of Roman rule in Britain, a series of 500 beacons was lit along the length of the wall. 13 March 2010
From geograph.org.uk. Author Gary Dickson

In AD 84 a fortress at Inchtuthil was dismantled before it was even finished and the fortifications of the Gask Ridge in Perthshire, erected in the wake of Mons Graupius, were abandoned within a few years. Troop numbers in Britannia were reduced accordingly and defence and consolidation rather than expansion was now the policy. Under Hadrian (r. 117 to 138) and Antoninus Pius (r. 138 to 161), two walls were built to deter and keep out the belligerent Caledonians. A line stretching across modern Northumberland from Newcastle-upon-Tyne to Carlisle on the Solway was the new limit of empire, a line which, constructed in the 120s and 130s AD, we know as Hadrian's Wall. This monumental barrier extended 73 miles comprising ditch, a thicket of spikes, a stone wall, a sequence of forts, mile castles and observation turrets, and a permanent garrison of up to 8,000 men. Other Roman army units were stationed further south – in bleak auxiliary forts in the Welsh mountains, the Pennines, the Yorkshire Moors and Wolds, or in the Lakes, the Southern Uplands of modern Scotland; or indeed in one of the three legionary

Spectacular Hardknott (Mediobogdum) Roman fort in the Lake District clearly showing bathhouse and parade ground; it is built on a rocky spur at 800'. Photographer Markas1370

Antonine Wall near Bar Hill; photographer: PaulT (Gunther Tschuch)

fortresses at Isca Silurium (Caerleon), Deva (Chester) and Eboracum (York).

The Antonine Wall was begun in 142, extending from the Firth of Forth to the Firth of Clyde. This was abandoned after twenty years and only occasionally re-occupied.

There were, nevertheless, sporadic incursions into Scotland when Roman troops penetrated deep into the north of the country several more times. Indeed, there were more Roman marching camps in Scotland than anywhere else in Europe as a result of at least four major attempts to subdue the area.

The Severan Reforms

Around AD 197, the Severan Reforms divided Britain into two provinces: Britannia Superior and Britannia Inferior. Emperor Septimius Severus (r. 193–211) arrived in Britain in 208, allegedly irritated by the bellicose Maeatae tribe, and waged war against the Caledonian Confederacy, a coalition of Brittonic Pictish tribes.

He deployed a formidable force: the three legions of the British garrison reinforced by the recently formed 2nd Parthica legion, 9,000 imperial guards with cavalry support, and numerous auxiliaries landed by the British fleet, the Rhine fleet and two fleets transferred from the Danube for the purpose. According to Dio Cassius, he ruthlessly committed acts of genocide against the natives and incurred the loss of 50,000 of his own men to guerrilla tactics before being forced to withdraw to Hadrian's Wall. He thoroughly repaired and reinforced the wall, reoccupied the Antonine Wall and invaded Caledonia. But he fell fatally ill in late 210 and died in early 211 at Eboracum. He was succeeded by his fractious sons, Caracalla and Geta.

York as *colonia* and the Diocletian Reforms

In the early third century York was granted the status of a Roman *colonia* while nearby Isurium Brigantum (Aldborough) expanded to become the largest civilian settlement in the region. During the Diocletian Reforms (Diocletian r.284 to 305) at the end of the third century, Constantius Chlorus I (*c*.250–306), was Roman co-emperor from 293 to 306 as part of the tetrarchy. As *Caesar*, or junior emperor, in 296 Constantius quelled the usurper Allectus who headed the spurious 'Britannic Empire'. Britannia was then further divided into four or five provinces under the direction of a *vicarius* (at Londinium), who administered what then became the Diocese of the Britains which was incorporated into the Prefecture of Gaul. The provinces seem to have been called Prima, Secunda, Maxima Caesariensis, and (possibly) Flavia Caesariensis and Valentia. York remained the administrative centre of Britannia Secunda.

Constantine the Great

On becoming *Augustus* in 305, Constantius launched a successful punitive campaign against the Picts beyond the Antonine Wall. However, he too died suddenly in Eboracum in 306. Before he did, however, Constantius recommended his son to the army as his successor; consequently Constantine was declared emperor by the legions at York.

Marble bust of the Emperor Constantine I, found before 1823, in Stonegate. Here he is clean-shaven and wears an imperial oak wreath; weathering suggests that he originally stood in the open, perhaps in front of the Headquarters Building of the legionary fortress? Date *c*.306–37. In the Yorkshire Museum; YORYM: 1998.23 Image © and courtesy of York Museums Trust

Constantine outside the Minster – the building which was built on his fortress

Constantine the Great was crowned Roman Emperor here and went on to establish the foundations of Roman Christendom.

The emperor Constantine died on the southern shores of the Gulf of Nicomedia (present-day Gulf of İzmit) in 337 – he was the first emperor to adopt the Christian faith, beginning the ending of the persecution of Christians in the Roman Empire in what was known as the Triumph of the Church, the Peace of the Church, or the Constantinian Shift. In 313, Constantine and Licinius issued the Edict of Milan decriminalizing Christian worship throughout the Roman empire. Religious tolerance, of a sort, had arrived. We have a document noting the attendance of Bishop Eborius of Eboracum (one of the three British bishops to attend) at the influential Council of Arles in 314 at which, amongst other things, the vexed date of Easter was fixed. The Episcopal see at Eboracum was called *Eboracensis* in Latin, and Bishops from the see also attended the equally influential First Council of Nicaea in 325, the Council of Sardica, and the Council of Ariminum. Not long before his death in May 337, Constantine was baptised into the Arian version of Christianity.

A small bone plaque possibly with Christian associations uncovered from an inhumation grave bore the phrase SOROR AVE VIVAS IN DEO ('Hail sister may you live in God').

The social situation

For much of the later period of the Roman occupation, Britannia was harassed and threatened by persistent barbarian invasions and often came under the temporary sway of imperial usurpers and bogus pretenders.

Typically, settlements of craftsmen, artisans, traders and motley camp followers grew up around the forts, provisioned by army contracts and soldiers' disposable pay. Local farms supplied grain, meat, leather, wool, beer, and other staples.

But, despite Tacitus' carping in the early years of the occupation about native indulgences, Roman Britain was never a luxurious place for the majority of the occupied north country natives: the land was impoverished, and the army always came first, taking what little surplus there was.

Nevertheless, these communities, *vici*, continued to spring up around the various military installations, as did roads, bridges and villas. Increasingly, a town in Britannia meant geometric street grids, forums (market squares), basilicas (assembly rooms), temples, theatres, bathhouses, amphitheatres, shopping arcades, taverns, cook shops, potteries, brothels and hotels. Mosaics, frescos and Roman ceramics, statues and gardens reflected the relative affluence of the nouveau riche Britons.

Why did the Romans invade Britannia anyway?

Why did the Romans feel the need to conquer Britannia? After all, the empire already stretched from the Sahara to the north German plains, from the Caucasus to the English Channel, and the Channel was a good, natural, defendable frontier. A cautious Augustus had reined in the hunger for booty – lucrative conquest – so rampant in the later Republic. It was increasingly hard to come by and he had learnt sobering lessons from the humiliating and costly massacre in the Teutoburger Wald in AD 9, and before that from the lesser-known Clades Lolliana in 17 BC, in which tribes led by the Sugambri from near what is now the Dutch–German border, defeated a Roman legion under the command of Marcus Lollius.

Augustus wielded complete control over what had now become the Roman empire; he also retained control of the Roman army – essentially to prevent a return to the bloody turmoil of the civil wars by covetous, power-hungry, often out of control, generals. He maintained a policy of limited expansion, largely keeping the new Empire within its existing borders. This was in the face of encouragement to invade Britannia to the west and Parthia in the east and a need to ensure that the legions were usefully employed to the benefit of the political establishment and Rome's stability rather than to their detriment. As far as the Romans could see, there was little out there now which would earn a return on expensive military campaigns; lucrative booty and fertile lands not under Roman control were now in short supply beyond the empire. Why bother? Augustus had the financial resources to satisfy and resettle veterans out of his substantial windfalls from the Ptolemaic empire; he was naturally unwilling to allow ambitious commanders any opportunity to fuel insurrection on the back of victorious and lucrative military campaigns.

Britain was relatively rich in resources such as copper, gold, iron, lead, salt, silver and tin, all in high demand in the Roman Empire. The Romans could depend on advanced technology to find, develop and extract valuable minerals on a scale unparalleled again until the later Middle Ages. But economics was not really a viable motive or an incentive – the Roman Empire already enjoyed riches-a-plenty and the natural resources in Britannia were not going to increase those reserves by very much.

The answer to why the Romans invaded was more to do with politics and celebrity than anything else. The emperor reigning at the time of the invasion, Claudius, was almost an emperor by default: the assassination of his predecessor, Caligula, left no obvious successor. Despite his undoubted intelligence and literary skills, Claudius has been portrayed as a bit of a buffoon (largely thanks to Robert Graves), an imperial embarrassment. He was in desperate need of an action, an event on an imperial, global scale, which would raise his political stock. Britannia was an obvious target, and so the invasion was on.

The Roman occupation of Britannia lasted until about AD 410, some 350 years after the Claudian invasion, when issues of international security demanded the return of troops to safeguard the very seats of empire. Ex-provinces like Britannia became increasingly dilapidated, but in the decades and centuries before, Britannia had developed politically, militarily, economically and socially.

One of the cities at the centre of this extended civilising process was Eboracum, whose inspirational story is documented and depicted in the following pages.

Hermannsdenkmal (1875), in Lippe, Germany, a huge copper memorial to Arminius and his Teutoburger Wald victory of the Romans between Paderborn and Gütersloh. Arminius must have reared up in the Roman consciousness when Boudica started her war in Britannia

Recent excavations and what we learn from them: 1970–2020

The city walls, the legionary bath-house and headquarters building, civilian houses, workshops, storehouses and cemeteries have all been excavated to a greater or lesser extent. In the 1950s archaeology was still an haphazard affair carried out by enthusiastic volunteers. However, in York, things changed immeasurably when Peter Wenham completed a number of digs with excellent results. They included the Davygate shopping arcade site from 1955 to 1958 where he revealed and recorded the fortress defences and four legionary barrack blocks (S, P, Q and R). His greatest achievement, however, was the excavation at Trentholme Drive in 1951–2 and 1957–9, south-west of Micklegate Bar where he uncovered a substantial Roman cemetery, the first in York to be tackled systematically and archaeologically. Peter Wenham was later joined in his endeavours by the Royal Commission on Historical Monuments for England (RCHME), working on a priceless inventory of the city. The first volume, *Eboracum*, was published in 1962 and lives on as a vital resource for research into Roman York.

The perilous state of an increasingly unstable central tower at York Minster and the unsuccessful quest for the Anglo-Saxon Minster referred to by Bede as the site of King Edwin of Northumbria's baptism in 627 prompted more fortress-focused excavations between 1967 and 1972, this time by Derek Philips. These resulted in a huge revelation which shed light on the story of the headquarters, basilica and barracks from the first to the fifth century.

The work of the RCHME duly moved on to Volume 2 and the city's defences. This allowed Jeffrey Radley to re-excavate a stone tower built into the Roman fortress wall close to the Multangular Tower. This was first discovered in 1842 when the Recorder of York, in cavalier fashion, drove a tunnel through the walls to access his stables in King's Manor. Radley attributed the tower to the post-Roman period and it assumed the name the 'Anglian Tower', although it is now considered to be late Roman. From 1971 it has been on display for all to see along with an adjacent stretch of the fortress wall exposed by removing the overlying medieval rampart.

Sadly, it seemed that very few people, if any, were listening or re-listening to a prophetic Willliam Etty when in the early nineteenth century he cautioned the decision makers of York to

> *Beware how you destroy your antiquities, guard them with religious care! They are what give you a decided character and superiority over other provincial cities. You have lost much, take care of what remains*

and urged them to spurn what has been called 'the destroying hand of progress'.

York archaeology remained haphazard and unco-ordinated at best; it was a flaccid response to the constant threat posed by the wrecking ball and bulldozers. What York so desperately needed was a co-ordinating body which wielded power and influence in pursuit of a viable strategy for 'rescue archaeology' which would ensure its involvement in and around future developments.

Things came to a head in 1968 with the publication of Lord Esher's landmark report *York: A Study in Conservation* which paved the way for plans for an inner ring-road. Above-ground historic buildings were largely safe but subterranean archaeology just outside the city walls including Roman cemeteries and suburbs were very much at risk. The cavalry arrived just in time when the Council for British Archaeology and the Yorkshire Philosophical Society underwrote the formation of the York Archaeological Trust (YAT), set up in April 1972. Initially

A YAT excavation at Bedern Hall in the early 1970s

under the aegis of Trust Director, Peter Addyman, the study of Roman York has been advanced immeasurably by their painstaking work; with their involvement and the participation of other like-minded bodies our knowledge is increasing all the time. The findings of the following excavations owe a tremendous amount to YAT and similarly motivated organisations.

No 9 Blake Street – barrack buildings inside the fortress 1975

This dig exposed parts of the fortress barrack building including the rear wall of the building, the residential block, a cobbled street, floors and the kitchen range, identified by a series of hearths used for cooking. Barracks for ordinary ranks were usually ranged along the perimeter of a fortress; typically, as here, they housed a century in ten pairs of rooms with each pair housing eight soldiers. The residential space was later divided into four rooms, possibly indicating a change of use. The centurion and his dependants lived in rooms at the end of the block. Mid-second-century rubbish tips here contained numerous nails, discarded, one can assume, when stone replaced the timber buildings.

Interestingly, 35 silver coins were excavated in the residential block dating from 66 BC to AD 79; this end date is some 70 years earlier than the date for construction given by pottery finds and suggests that the hoard was possibly a votive offering. Just as mysterious but much more macabre was the discovery of an infant skeleton under the floor, as discussed below.

No. 5 Rougier Street – a building which was probably a warehouse in the *colonia*, 1981

The 1981 excavations on the corner of Rougier Street and Tanner Row (where the Malmaison Hotel now is) near the main approach road to York from the south-west have been especially productive: it has yielded a plethora of evidence for buildings and artefacts including remains of late second-century timber buildings complete with refuse heaps which offered up 3 metres of Roman deposits and 'confirmed the existence of a mature Roman urban landscape'. This was followed in 1983–4 by more extensive archaeology nearby.

Nos 21–22 Wellington Row – second-century stone building in the *colonia* of uncertain use

This excavation delivered 4 metres of superimposed layers below the road comprising layers of turf and hazel branches with nuts below the earliest layer. They were rejected as preparation for the road as this usually takes the form of wattle, turf and strong timbers. The hazel branches were probably a sort of religious offering thanking the gods for the use of the road, a notion supported by the discovery of an alder bowl in the same site.

Wellington Row may have been the site of one of York's earliest floods; why else build up the road level by 1 metre with a mound of large cobbles covered with layers of packed gravel? The Wellington Row building was some size: 15.5 metres x 10.5 metres situated on the main road from the south east. A clay oven was found against one of the walls as well as a pillar composed of three millstone grit blocks. Like Rougier Street the building had been burnt in a fire – probably the same fire. The fire at Wellington Row had turned the walls pink and bright red.

The reconstruction after the fire involved an extension of 2 metres with 200 timber piles driven into the base, mainly oak logs. Four pits were found dug into the floor – three contained pots, the other a glass bowl. One of the pots was found in a wooden box filled with fish bones – no doubt the detritus from a fish sauce (*garum*) making session. The burial of pots probably suggests a votive offering to the *genius loci*. We can only speculate on the purpose of the building – it was neither a dwelling nor a workshop but it may have been a meeting hall for a *collegium* or merchant guild – rather like the mediaeval Merchant Adventurers' Hall we can still see today. A number of bone combs and a jet plaque from the fourth century have been uncovered.

Tanner Row (General Accident) – second-century timber building and stone building late third century, 1983–4

The so-called General Accident site was one of the first York rescue excavations to receive significant funding from the site developers. Two stone pillars found here would suggest they supported a warehouse as it was customary to raise such buildings off the ground to deter vermin and allow the free circulation of air to reduce damp. A large deposit of burnt material – mainly grain with some charred timbers – was also revealed. This deposit also yielded a small stone relief depicting a cockerel with bags on its back; it is beneath a pair of feet – Mercury's feet? Mercury, messenger god, with cockerel is a familiar feature in Roman art; he was also associated with the protection of merchants. Maybe Mercury's messages were in the little bags. The grain deposits comprised 89 per cent spelt wheat (*Triticum spelta*) and 11 per cent barley – this was probably used in brewing. The site is notable for what this dig revealed about second-century timber buildings and for the treasure-trove refuse heaps. The earlier excavation was followed up with further work from May 1988, which elided into …

Wellington Row/Tanner Row – road from the south west leading to possible site of a Roman bridge over the Ouse.

A large stone building was found to have been built on the side of this road with a history extending from the late second to the fourth century. It offers, then, a useful, practical timeline for much of Roman York generally. The site also shows the continuation of a roadside ditch evident at Rougier Street and Wellington Street with a cobbled yard at one end; dung enriched with hay would suggest that horses or cattle were kept here, a theory reinforced by the discovery of insects which commonly infested stables. Parasites were instrumental in confirming the presence in a drain here of kitchen waste and human faeces – numerous eggs of parasite worms found in the human gut were unearthed.

This organic matter and much more like it may well be indicative of a changing ecological environment in York about this time – assisted, of course, by the unusual ubiquity of waterlogged ground which preserves organic matter. As the population grew and human activity became increasingly established over time, so did the mark we left on the urban environment. Archaeologists are digging up more and more evidence of this footprint all the time and although it teaches us a prodigious amount about Roman life it does, at the same time, give pause for thought – environmental destruction is by no means a twenty-first-century blight. Food leftovers and waste, faeces from humans and domestic animals, general litter, cereal detritus, hay – all contributed to the general mess that was gradually building up. This in turn was a magnet for pests: flies in house and stable, fleas, dung beetles, mice, black rats (*rattus rattus*) – plague carriers in the Middle Ages – were all swarming round, to say nothing of the scavenging bird life and feral dogs and cats. All of this would have had a negative impact on public health with disease increasing in the face of increasingly squalid conditions and sanitation. Even the Romans presided over an environmental disaster waiting to happen.

Evidence reveals significant artisan activity around the General Accident site, metalworking being particularly well represented. All the signs are there: slag from ironworking, and copper working; metal scrap in abundance and iron tools. Leather off-cuts and bits of shoe confirm the presence of leather working – a trade which persisted for many years in this area, hence Tanner Row; a sizeable fragment from an army tent and pieces from others have also been excavated. The VIth legion centurion and inveterate graffiti artist, Marcus Sollius Julianus must have been having a quiet day when he whiled away his time etching his name on one of the fragments; he turns up again on Hadrian's Wall, his name scratched onto a stone used by his men in the construction of the wall. Pieces of uniforms and an iron sword probably in for repair have also been found here.

Inside the city walls under the old railway station – evidence of a huge public baths complex.

The construction of the old station in 1839 did reveal evidence of the baths but only at the expense of the destruction of the Roman and medieval defences. We have already mentioned how this civic vandalism was described by Patrick Ottaway as 'perhaps the most devastating episode of destruction ever suffered by York's archaeology' but it is well worth repeating. Part of a bath house has also been found in Fetter Lane with IXth legion floor tiles.

The old station site has also delivered two bronze plaques with dedications in Greek by Scribonius Demetrius – one to the gods of the military commander's house and the other to Ocean and Tethys – a titan and titaness; Ocean was the divine personification of the ocean, which the Greeks perceived as an enormous river encircling the world, while Tethys, his wife, was mother of the river gods and the Oceanids. Demetrius, being a teacher, would have been familiar this mythology; indeed, he was privileged to meet Plutarch, the Roman biographer and historian, in Delphi in AD 83, fascinated to hear of his exploits on a journey to the 'western isles', beyond that awesome ocean encircling the known world. When Alexander the Great reached as far as the River Indus in 323 BC he dedicated altars to Oceanus and Tethys to mark the furthest point east he reached; Demetrius, no doubt, considered his feat of reaching the Western Isles an achievement of no less magnitude.

RIB 663

> Ὠκεανῶι
> καὶ Τηθύι
> Δημήτρι[ος]

To Ocean and Tethys Demetrius (set this up).

Junction of Micklegate (Nos 1–9) and Skeldergate – substantial early third-century bath house (Queen's Hotel), 1988–9

York's huge bath house with its 9,100 square metres is at the north-east end of Micklegate. The walls were a mighty 2.2 metres thick – as thick as Roman walls come in York – and up to 3.5 metres high. They each had arched openings which formed part of the hypocaust system. All was destroyed in the second half of the fourth century.

3 and 6 Driffield Terrace, 2004–5: the now world-famous 'gladiator' cemetery: 'The headless gladiators of York' as featured on TV.

This is covered in detail in the chapter on 'Burials'.

St Leonard's Hospital 2001–3

The site has uncovered more of one of the interval towers (SW6) as part of a training dig inspired by a three-day project in 1999 under the auspices of the TV programme, *Time Team*.

fortress SW defences (stone phase now dated to early second century)

Obviously when talking about the south-west defences the focus will be on the Multangular Tower; however, there is much more to this area, as shown in the relevant section of the walk around the visible remains in York at the beginning of the book.

Hungate 2006–12

This major archaeological excavation unveiled aspects of 2,000 years of York's history and was the largest developer-funded project to take place

YAT digging in Hungate

in York so far and the biggest urban excavation in the city for 25 years covering a 2,500 sq m (26,900 sq ft) area. York Archaeological Trust spent five years on the dig before handing the site back to developers. Hungate, near by the River Foss, has been under continuous occupation for most of the past 2,000 years. Part of the site contains the remains of an early Roman cemetery.

Project director Peter Connelly, said, 'It is the largest Roman cemetery excavated in York for a century. We've discovered amazing pieces of Roman jewellery.' These jewels include a Roman necklace consisting of 299 small glass beads and rare jet jewellery dating from the third or fourth centuries.

East Heslington (University of York), late 2000s

The excavations of the 115 hectare site of University of York campus expansion at Heslington East has yielded settlement evidence from the early Bronze Age through to Roman times. Particularly interesting is a late-Roman well excavated here; its construction, use and demise is described in a 2013 paper published in *Internet Archaeology* entitled 'A Late Roman Well at Heslington East, York: ritual or routine practices' by Steve Roskams et al. This tells us a lot about the Romans' use of wells, their diet and butchery.

1067 animal bone fragments were recovered from the well; the proportion of gnawed bones was low, while burnt bones were extremely rare; there was a very high proportion of butchered bone; 14 of its 39 horse bones were butchered. The paper goes on to tell us that 'other deposits [nearby] contained a partial dog skeleton recovered from a late Roman ditch; a pig skeleton from a late Roman pit; and a sheep/goat skeleton'.

476 fragments were found in the third fill (although 159 were of frogs/toads, likely 'pitfall' victims). A horse skull and two horned cattle skulls were found here; disarticulated bones from all body parts were discovered from cattle and horses. All major body parts from both are represented. Of the cattle bones, 25 were butchered, including damage to three scapulae associated with hook damage during smoking, and skinning marks on a metacarpal. Six horse bones also exhibited dismembering marks.

The fourth fill yielded a red deer skeleton and skeletons of a dog (Skeleton 2). The archaeologists determined that

> the deer skeleton is from a sub-adult individual between 13 and 16 months old. Based on an early summer birth, this animal was hunted in the summer or autumn of its second year. In the absence of any antlers or antler buds, it is presumably female. Cut marks to its left humerus indicate that the carcass was processed to some extent, although with all body parts present the animal was clearly not dismembered and its joints widely distributed … This fill also contained a pole-axed cattle skull from an adult animal and a large, complete red deer antler from an impressively

large and mature stag, both clearly contrasting with the age at death of deer, dog and calf.

Roskams, S., Neal, C., Richardson, J. and Leary, R., 'A Late Roman Well at Heslington East, York: ritual or routine practices?'[1]

The Roman Camp at Huntington South Moor (2003)

Two camps were identified from aerial photography in 2002; Camp 1 was excavated at length in the following year revealing that the camp had been marked out very precisely. The camp covered 1.55 ha., big enough to accommodate 500 or so troops. The camp was used in the first half of the second century but soon slighted. A full report by Mark Stiles Johnson was published in *York Historian* 29 (2012).

28–40 Blossom Street

Excavations in 2009 revealed varied activities had taken place on the site. These included farming, waste disposal, occupation and perhaps a cremation cemetery. The findings are discussed in the context of land use outside the *vicus* with a reassessment of the local Roman road system. A full report by Ian Milsted was published in *York Historian* 27 (2010).

Newington Hotel 2017/18 cemetery adjacent to the Trentholme Drive site

The redevelopment of the former Newington Hotel gave York Archaeological Trust a chance to explore and study an important aspect of York's Roman past.

The site is on Mount Vale, only about 200 yards from where YAT uncovered the Headless Roman skeletons of Driffield Terrace; it is part

---

[1] Internet Archaeology (2013): 34. https://doi.org/10.11141/ia.34.5

of a Roman cemetery that was first excavated by Peter Wenham on the neighbouring Trentholme Drive site in the 1950s – one of the first Romano-British burial grounds to be fully published in the UK.

Three months into the dig and some 75 graves were recorded. The graves were mostly very shallow – something that Wenham had also noted– indicating that many of them had been plough damaged throughout the medieval period and nineteenth-century construction.

YAT tells us that

> At first glance, the image is decidedly chaotic: rather than lying in regimented rows the graves crowd together, oriented towards all points of the compass and frequently intercutting. As for who was buried there, this was a demographically diverse cemetery, populated by both men and women, and individuals of all ages from infants to elderly adults – although they seem to have been broadly of the same social class.
>
> Nor was there anything immediately spectacular about the objects that accompanied these everyday individuals to the grave – only two contained any items of personal adornment. One grave yielded a jet pin, while another individual had been interred wearing some kind of copper alloy head ornament whose flaky, corroded remains had left a green stain on their forehead. Otherwise, grave goods were limited to pots, which were found interred with young and old alike.[2]

The search for the missing amphitheatre, King's Manor, 2017

It may not just be Richard III who suffered the indignity of being found buried under a city car park. York's undiscovered amphitheatre may

---

2   https://www.yorkarchaeology.co.uk/case-studies-blog/2019/6/3/excavating-eboracums-common-people

also be languishing under a similar car park. The other British legionary fortresses, Chester and Caerleon, each boast an amphitheatre, and a cemetery on the Mount appears to have been the burial ground for scores of gladiators. As yet firm archaeological evidence for an amphitheatre in Eboracum remains elusive. It may, though, be under the car park at King's Manor. Stewart Ainsworth, Chester University archaeologist and part of Channel 4's *Time Team* fame asserts: '[York is] a massive legionary presence. It should have an amphitheatre – it will have one, it just hasn't been found in my opinion.'

Tim Sutherland, a lecturer on battlefields and archaeology at the University of York, also became convinced that the King's Manor site could have been where the amphitheatre lies when he noticed that the surrounding buildings had over the years tilted in the direction of a depression. 'We need to know what the hollow is,' he said. 'We are hoping to start something that could become very big news indeed.' The team

The excavated amphitheatre at Chester from Newgate showing the curved road that surrounds the perimeter; something similar may yet come to light in York. Author: Nadia from Sydney, Australia. OpenStreetMap data and maps are licensed under the Creative Commons Attribution-ShareAlike 2.0 license (CC-BY-SA 2.0)

used ground-penetrating radar to look underneath King's Manor for any evidence of the amphitheatre.

Other finds in York include a stone fountain unearthed in Bishophill in 1906 – now unfortunately dismantled; a timber-lined 6-metre-deep well at 58–59 Skeldergate, which was probably used for gardens as well as for drinking if the box clippings (tidy, aromatic and curative) found inside are anything to go by; plaster showing human figures and plants at 37 Bishophill Senior. A Roman well languishes under the stage in York Theatre Royal.

We have already mentioned how in 1972 a Roman sewer was discovered on the north side of Church Street in which copious amounts of waste water from the baths and latrines would have been washed away. If the baths at Exeter are comparable then something like 70,000 gallons gushed though a day. It extended for 44 metres and was high enough to allow slaves to crawl along inside to clean it.

The sponge on a stick

What with all those public baths, latrines with washing facilities, sewer systems, fountains and clean drinking water from aqueducts you would think that the Romans (at least the comfortably off ones) would have enjoyed a reasonable level of personal hygiene and were largely free from chronic stomach upsets. Not a bit of it; research led by Piers Mitchell from the Department of Archaeology and Anthropology of the University of Cambridge, and published in the journal *Parasitology,* found that baths and the like did nothing to protect the Romans from those annoying, embarrassing parasites.

Mitchell and his team rolled up their sleeves and used archaeological evidence from cesspits, sewer drains, rubbish pits, burials and other sites to assess the impact of parasites across Roman Europe, the Middle East and North Africa.

Unfortunately for the Romans, analysis of all of the above plus ancient latrines, human burials and coprolites (fossilized faeces) clearly demonstrated that, instead of decreasing as expected, intestinal parasites actually increased compared with the preceding Iron Age.

'The impressive sanitation technologies introduced by the Romans did not seem to have delivered the health benefits that we would expect,' Mitchell said. He found that the most widely spread intestinal parasites in the Roman Empire were whipworm (*Trichuris trichiura*) and roundworm (*Ascaris lumbricoides*) which are transmitted by the contamination of food with faeces. 'It could have been spread by the use of unwashed hands to prepare food or by the use of human faeces as crop fertilizer,' Mitchell concluded. Also prolific was *Entamoeba histolytica*, a protozoan that causes dysentery, with bloody diarrhoea, abdominal pain and fevers. It is contracted by drinking water contaminated by human faeces.

Ectoparasites such as lice and fleas were as common among so-called civilised Romans as in later Viking and medieval populations, where bathing was not so widely practised. Despite all their regular bathing and flushing latrines the Romans systematically undid all that good work by using as a substitute for toilet paper and for hand washing … a communal sponge on a stick.

The food chain was another culprit. 'Human and animal faeces were often used to fertilize crops, thus leading to reinfection of the population with intestinal parasites when they ate this food,' Mitchell said. The study also found fish tapeworm eggs surprisingly widespread in the Roman empire, in contrast to the evidence from the Bronze and Iron Ages. The ever-popular fermented fish sauce (*garum*) may not have helped: *garum* was made from pieces of fish, herbs, salt and flavourings but the sauce was not cooked, instead it was allowed to ferment in the sun. 'Fish tapeworm eggs could have been transported large distances across the empire in the *garum* sauce and then consumed,' Mitchell explained.

The big houses, villas and *mansiones,* continued to be built into the late third to early fourth century, evidenced by the remains of town houses decorated with mosaic pavements; for example at St Mary, Castlegate and in Aldwark, Bar Lane, Toft Green and Clementhorpe. A good example of a town house is in Bishophill, built in the late third century with at least two ranges of rooms around a courtyard.

Fortress York: from wooden fort to *Colonia*

In many respects, as Hargrove more than hints, York is the jewel in the crown of Roman Britain. The legionary fortress was established in AD 71 on land north-east of the River Ouse in the traditional playing card plan, occupying about 25 hectares. It was the largest town in northern Britain and, in time, capital city of Britannia Inferior. There was nothing 'inferior' about this place though – the adjective simply meant northern Britain – but it may well have been a starting point for the enduring fallacy that the south is superior in some way to the north.

Vespasian was already a veteran of Britannia; he became emperor in the fall-out from the turbulent Year of the Four Emperors in AD 69. Once he had quelled uprisings in Judaea and the Netherlands he appointed Q. Petillius Cerialis (ca. AD 30 – after AD 83) governor of Britannia; Cerialis, a relative of Vespasian, was accompanied by the II *Adiutrix* from Nijmegen which he stationed at Lincoln. He was supported by Gnaeus Julius Agricola, commander of XX *Valeria Victrix*.

Cerialis had his first experience of Britannia as legate of Legio IX *Hispana* under governor Gaius Suetonius Paulinus. In the Boudican rebellion Cerialis suffered a serious reverse when attempting to relieve the city of Camulodunum (Colchester), which was taken by the Britons before he arrived. Tacitus says, 'The victorious enemy met Petillius Cerialis, commander of the ninth legion, as he was coming to the rescue, routed his troops, and destroyed all his infantry. Cerialis escaped with some cavalry into the camp, and was saved by its fortifications.'[3]

---

3 (Tacitus *Annals* 14, 32)

The Romans pushed north from the Humber in AD 71 when the local incumbents, the Brigantes, became restless; Cerialis led the IXth legion north from Lincoln to found Eboracum, initially a wooden fort built perhaps as a temporary measure while the Romans monitored the sitiation with the Brigantes.

The drive into the north of England is identifiable by what the Romans built on the way: Lincoln, York and Stanwick were the power points while Brough on the Humber guarded the Humber crossing and the flanks were defended from the east Yorkshire Parisi at Malton and Hayton. A day's march separated legionary camps at Rey Cross, Crackenthorpe and Plumpton Head.

The original wooden camp at York was refurbished by Agricola in 81 and was completely rebuilt in stone between 107 and 108. The early second century saw the start of more long-term rebuilding under Trajan but extending for a century or so into the reign of Septimius Severus.

Model of the timber tower of the fortress after Agricola's rebuild in AD 81 based on excavations in Davygate in 1955. Originally published in Herman Ramm's *Roman York* (1991)

Something like over 48,000m³ of stone was used – mainly magnesian limestone from the quarries at Calcaria, Tadcaster. The Romans used several other types of stone in their buildings including millstone grit and Elland stone (York stone), which was used for floors and roofs as it splits naturally into flat slabs. However, the use of mortar to hold everything together was the real Roman revolution enabling far larger buildings than ever seen before.

As befits its high military and political status, Eboracum was visited by the emperors of the day. Hadrian came in 122 en route to his great wall project, bringing with him the VIth legion to replace the incumbent IXth.

Septimius Severus arrived in 208, using the fortress as his base for his Scottish campaign. The Imperial court was based in York until at least 211 when Severus died and was succeeded by his sons, Caracalla and Geta. Severus was cremated in Eboracum.

The later third century saw the western Empire embroiled in political and economic turmoil with Britannia some time ruled by usurpers independent of Rome. Emperor Constantius I subdued these pretenders and came to Eboracum in 306, with the unfortunate reputation of becoming the second Emperor to die here. 'See York and die,' they must

This what the soldiers from the VIth would have found in Britannia

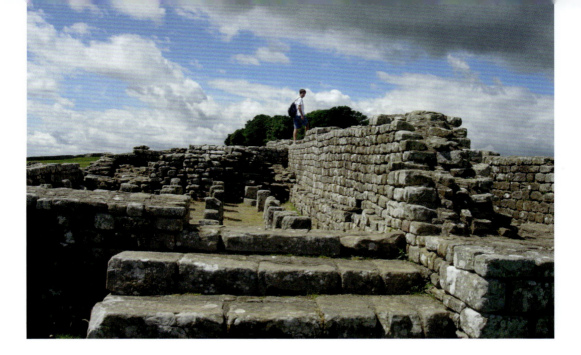

Granary at Housesteads on Hadrian's Wall, photograph taken by Mark A. Wilson (Department of Geology, The College of Wooster, Ohio). Author, Wilson44691 at English Wikipedia

have pondered back in Rome. His son Constantine was proclaimed as successor by the troops in the fortress. It has long been thought that Constantine rebuilt the south-west front of the fortress with polygonally-fronted interval towers and the two great corner towers, one of which – the Multangular Tower – still stands today in all its glory. However, rebuilding of the defences in the third and fourth centuries is now doubted. The Multangular Tower is now thought to date to the early second century, and this dating probably applies to the entire south-west stone defences.

As noted, Eboracum, was *the* major military base in the north of Britain; politically it was just as important: after the third century division of Britannia, it was the capital of northern Britain, Britannia Inferior. By 237 Eboracum was elevated to a *colonia*, the highest legal status any Roman city could attain, one of only four confirmed in Britain. At around the same time Eboracum became self-governing, with a council made up of affluent local merchants, and veteran soldiers. In 296 Britannia Inferior was divided further into two provinces of equal status with Eboracum the provincial capital of Britannia Secunda.

The magnificent second-century Multangular Tower

One of the Vindolanda tablets gives us our earliest written reference to York, datable to about AD 100, occurring as Eburacum, as it does in the *Antonine Itinerary* and seventh-century *Ravenna Cosmography*, two Roman 'road atlases' which list place-names along the highways of the empire. The Vindolanda reference is one of thirty or so literary and epigraphic references to York. The form Eboracum is more common, occurring, for example, in the works of the second century Greek geographer Ptolemy and on several stone inscriptions from York.

Constantine outside the Minster

A LIFE IN THE DAY OF A ROMAN IN YORK I: OFF TO THE BATHS IN THE EARLY SECOND CENTURY AD

Gaius Octavius Tidius Tossianus Lucius Javolenus Priscus – we'll just call him Javolenus – was a prominent Roman senator and jurist who flourished during the Flavian dynasty. Many of his judgments are quoted in the Digest.[4] *Priscus served as consul for September–December AD 86 as the colleague of Aulus Bucius Lappius Maximus. He took command of Legio IV Flavia Felix, stationed near Burnum, in modern Croatia and then served as the* de facto *governor of Numidia, modern Algeria. He was next appointed* legatus *or commander of Legio III Augusta in 83. It was in 84 when Javolenus Priscus came to Britain and served as a* juridicus *(senior judge) remaining here for two years. Of the many citations of his legal opinions, one concerns the will of Seius Saturninus,* archigubernus ex classe Britannica *(chief navigator in the British fleet), a case which must have come before him while he was* juridicus *in Britain.*

Javolenus Priscus was glad to finish his day at the Basilica courts. Now he could relax, starting with a well-earned visit to the baths. So he got in his litter and headed for the nearest bath house where he would meet some friends, learn the latest news and re-emerge a new man.

The baths and bathing were an essential facet of Roman life for men, women and children, rich and poor, slaves and free. Some very rich

---

4   The prestigious *Digest* is a digest of juristic writings on Roman law compiled by order of Justinian I in AD 530–33

Romans had their own baths in their sumptuous houses but most Romans availed themselves of the public baths. Baths were everywhere – as ubiquitous as temples, brothels and bars – and in Rome were said to number 856 no less in Javolenus' day. Socialising in the baths was as routine as worshipping in those temples or drinking in those bars. Baths, with their conviviality and their often splendid architecture, were just good places to be; indeed, Javolenus Priscus could think of nowhere better to be as he paid his nominal entrance fee and entered the *thermae*. What Javolenus really liked was the fact that the baths were a micro version of Rome itself with its shops, massage rooms, *palaestrae* or gymnasiums and rest rooms, covered promenades; some top-end baths even boasted libraries, museums, and gardens. Pure civilisation.

But there were disadvantages, particularly if, like Seneca the Younger, you had the misfortune to live in a flat above a public bath house; in this letter to Lucilius he reveals a fascinating glimpse into what went on in these places:

> Imagine what a din reverberates in my ears! I have lodgings right over a bathing establishment. So picture the assortment of sounds, which are so loud as to make me hate my very powers of hearing! When your strongman, for example, is exercising himself by wielding lead weights, when he is working hard, or else pretends to be working hard, I can hear him grunt, and whenever he exhales his imprisoned breath, I can hear him panting, wheezy and hissing. Or perhaps I notice some lazy fellow, content with a cheap rubdown, and hear the crack of the pummeling hand on his shoulder, varying in sound according to whether that hand is laid on a flat or hollow part of the body … Add to this the arrest of the odd drunk or pickpocket, the noise of the man who always likes to sing out loud in the bath, or the over-keen men who plunge into the swimming pool splashing loudly. Besides all of these … picture the hair-plucker with his penetrating, shrill voice which he uses for self-advertising, – continually giving it vent and never shutting up except when he is plucking armpits and making his victim scream instead. Then the cake seller with his various cries, the sausage man, the sweet seller, and all the vendors of food hawking their wares, each with his own individual yell.

Seneca the Younger, *Letters* 56, 1, 2

Theft was a major problem too. Javolenus recelled how, when he was serving in Britannia, he would go to the baths at Aquae Sulis [Bath] where a number of curse tablets were displayed excoriating thieves who stole bathers' possessions. These were 'prayers for justice', for thefts of and restitution for thefts of jewellery, gemstones, money, household goods and clothing. The inscriptions declared that the stolen property was transferred to a deity (Sulis) so that the loss is actually the deity's loss; the suspect is named and, often, the victim; the victim then invites the deity to visit afflictions on the thief, including death, not as a punishment but to induce the thief to return the stolen items. One which Javolenus particularly remembers went:

> Solinus, to the goddess Sulis Minerva. I give to your divinity and majesty [my] bathing costume and cloak. Do not allow sleep or health to him who has done me wrong, whether man or woman or whether slave or free unless he reveals himself and brings those goods to your temple.

And – cursing the thief with insanity and blindness:

> Docimedis has lost two gloves and asks that the thief responsible should lose their minds and eyes in the goddess' temple.

To be on the safe side, Javolenus tipped the clothing attendant anyway.

The procedure in the baths was very logical: Javolenus dropped his clothes off at the *apodyterium* or changing room and went straight into the *sudatoria* to work up a sweat and then the *frigidarium* – the cold water bath or swimming pool; he then progressed to the *tepidarium* or warm room, followed by the *caldarium* or a hot-water bath, sauna or steam room with its under-floor hypocaust heating courtesy of a brazier burning beneath the hollow floor. He then went back to the *tepidarium* to enjoy a massage with oils scraped off with a strigil.

A whole army of beauty and grooming specialists was on hand to pander to his needs: Martial notes the *tractatrix* – the masseuse who spreads her practiced hand (*manus docta*) over every limb, the *unctores* (perfumers), *fricatores* (rubbers), *alipilarii* (depilators) and the *picatrices* – the girls who trimmed your pubic hair. The slaves then rubbed him down with towels made from the softest wool and wrapped him in a scarlet woollen cloak. Then it was to the *laconium* – a dry rest room to relax. Rest over, Javolenus went out into the *palaestra*, an open-air garden where he did some light exercise. Returning inside he bought a snack and some perfume and laid down to enjoy the marble mosaics on the floors, the stuccoed walls and their pastoral frescoes, the gold stars and celestial imagery up in the domes and the statuary and fountains. A perfect end to the day.

Mixed bathing was increasingly the norm in Javolenus' day, but in the Republic men and women bathers had been segregated.

The *palaestra* was very important to the Romans; it was where they could take exercise: Javolenus sometimes went there first for a workout before bathing. It was essentially a rectangular court surrounded by colonnades with rooms leading off for bathing, playing ball, just watching, or for storage of oil, dust for the hands and athletic equipment. Here too was where the wrestlers wrestled – men and women, although not together.

– adapted from *How to be a Roman – A life in the day of a Roman* family by Paul Chrystal, 2017.

The Roman baths at Bath

The early occupation and the fortress

The canonical date for the establishment of the Roman legionary fortress at York is AD 71 under the governorship of Quintus Petillius Cerialis. But there was significant military activity shortly before that which goes some way to explain what happened here from AD 71. We have archaeological evidence of a short-lived Roman base predating the fortress established under Vettius Bolanus, governor from 69–71.

We know that the Roman fortress was on the east side of the river, centred on where the Minster stands today, occupying a large diagonal space stretching from the corner of Lord Mayor's Walk and Gillygate to the Multangular Tower in Museum Gardens, then down parallel with the River Ouse to Jubbergate and up to the Merchant Taylor's Hall.

Reinforcing the fortress at Eboracum

The first defences consisted of ditch, rampart and timber structures. The four gates (*portae*) which gave access to the main roads leading in and out were made from timber and were simply gaps in the walls which were initially 3-metre-high ramparts made of timber, clay and turf. A palisade ran along the top of the rampart with look-out towers at regular intervals. The ramparts themselves were protected by ditches, the spoil from which was used to make the ramparts which were faced with turves.

In AD 80 these ramparts were strengthened with seasoned timbers onto which a new earth bank was erected, again with turf facing and a palisade complete with towers and encircled by a double ditch. Inside the buildings were timber framed with wattle and daub infill.

An inscription now in the Yorkshire Museum tells us that in AD 107–8 the south-east gate (at King's Square) was rebuilt in stone. We also know that the inner ditch was filled in around the same time using some of the original turves; it was replaced by a stone wall with stone towers. This was probably part of a general consolidation of all three legionary fortresses. Stronger foundations came in the early third century possibly in preparation for the visit of Severus. At the east corner the wall was 16 foot high and 6ft wide at its base, narrowing to 5ft at the top, all made of grouted rubble, faced inside and out with Tadcaster stone. A cobbled walk ran behind the wall on top of the earth bank at a lower level than the wall. Two ruinous internal towers can be seen adjoining the wall.

Inside, excavations have revealed timber buildings near St William's College and off Blake Street. The *principia* was first built of stone in the early second century and reinforced in the early fourth century under Constantine.

Roman fortresses tended to follow a template – outer ditch or ditches and a wooden palisade or stone wall to the front of an earth rampart separated by an area called the berm. The intervallum road ran inside all of this. York's fortress underwent a series of strengthenings.

1. AD 71 – Legio IX: temporary wooden fort surrounded by an outer ditch; wooden palisade and a turfed rampart. Wooden towers were erected at each corner and at regular intervals.
2. AD 81 – Legio IX: Eboracum was now deemed permanent and the AD 71 fort needed refurbishing anyway. So, another ditch was added with the spoil used to heighten and widen the rampart. Some towers were replaced; huge oak timbers have been excavated at Davygate – dendrochronologists have assessed that one of these came from a tree that was growing when Jesus was alive. More internal buildings made of wood.

A reconstructon of the Roman siege tower used at Masada, demonstrating the sort of hardware the Romans had at their disposal in other parts of the empire. Courtesy of Bibleplaces.com

3. AD 107–8 – Legio IX: the wooden palisade was replaced by a stone wall built to the front of a heightened and widened rampart. The original ditches were filled in and re-dug further away from the front of the stone wall. Wooden internal buildings replaced by stone.

We also know that the civilian city, the *vicus* or later *colonia*, on the other bank of the River Ouse – was roughly centred around present-day Rougier Street, North Street and George Hudson Street.

One of the most obvious signs of the Roman footprint were the physical defences they interlaced within any conquered territory in order to serve the needs of the Roman army; these included forts, milecastles, roads, signal stations, defensive walls and town walls.

Why did the Romans elect to construct a fortress here? York clearly benefitted from its site at the confluence of two rivers. However, it seems likely that the original strategy was for York to be only a temporary base from which to suppress the Brigantean insurgencies. As the Romans pushed north and achieved what looked like the final victory over the Britons at the Battle of Mons Graupius (AD 83), the Legio XX *Valeria Victrix* under Agricola, now governor from AD 77, moved north to Inchtuthil on the River Tay. However, barbarian threats to Rome meant a reallocation of imperial resources and the withdrawal of one legion from Britain; the Romans retreated to the Solway–Tyne isthmus which would later be consolidated into Hadrian's Wall. The result was that York became the permanent base for the northern-most army of imperial Rome.

As noted, the Brigantes were the local tribe and, to the east of York, the Parisi occupied a territory roughly in line with the former East Riding of Yorkshire. The new fortress was ideally placed to keep a close eye on these two tribes and to react to any trouble as required. York was pivotal to the consolidation and spread of the occupation and as a vital staging post for the supply and garrisoning of Hadrian's Wall. All roads led to and from York. Eboracum was there for the long haul, remaining as it did for the entirety of the Roman period.

Two of modern York's main streets, Stonegate and Petergate, more or less trace the line of the two principal streets in the fortress, the *via praetoria* and the *via principalis* so we can see how the layout of the fortress has determined the layout of the modern city. The *via praetoria* led to the south-west gate (*porta praetoria*) where St Helen's Square is now, revealing that the fortress faced south-west towards the River Ouse. The *via principalis* linked the gates on the north-west and south-east sides – the *portae principales* – on the sites of Bootham Bar and King's Square. The *porta decumana* – a rear gate central on the north-east sides – remains hidden under the mediaeval rampart.

The key buildings

Archaeological evidence remains tantalisingly sparse – much of it so near but so far, buried as it under the Minster. We know that York certainly had some of the following structures, others remain frustratingly elusive.

The HQ

The all important and imposing *principia* – headquarters building – was at the centre of a range of buildings surrounding a courtyard including, on the north-east side, a great aisled hall or basilica.

The basilica

The main building for local government and justice – usually aisled halls with a raised dais at one end reserved for trials and council meetings,

The column with the minster in the background built on where more such columns presumably lie in the basilica

a central hall and offices. To give some idea of the magnitude of these buildings, the basilica at York was larger than the Minster nave under the central tower extending diagonally across the south transept. There would have been 16 or so free standing columns, eight on each side, one of which (7.6 metre high), as noted, was unearthed in excavations under York Minster where it had fallen. It now stands outside the south door of the Minster. It was made from magnesian limestone and millstone grit, the former from Calcaria (Tadcaster), the grit from Bramham Park near Wetherby.

The forum

York's forum – the focus for all life for every Roman town – remains elusive. It was the go-to meeting place and was where elections were held, proclamations to the citizens were made and where business was conducted. They was usually an enclosed spaced open to the air which may have had colonnaded sides to allow business to be conducted in bad weather. In Britain this was usually rain, unlike many other countries in the Empire where the colonnade would provide shelter from the sun. Temporary stalls would have been clustered in and around the forum.

The *mansiones*

These were staging posts for those on official or military journeys but could also be used by commercial travellers. There were facilities for feeding horses and mules, stabling and shoeing. The buildings could be two storied and usually had a bath house attached. Examples are known at Silchester and Caerwent.

Water supply

The supply of fresh water to towns was an indicator of the sophistication of Roman civil engineering. Usually, water was brought in from fresh water rivers, and channelled underground in conduits, although a small number of aqueducts are known in Britain, the one at Lincoln is an example. The water was obviously used for drinking, domestic use and for bath houses. The need to drain the continually running excess water away led to the building of drains throughout Roman towns such as York. Water for most of the town was from wells; a good example has been excavated in Skeldergate and there is another under the stage at the Theatre Royal.

Shops and markets

The *macellum* was a covered market for trading and could be housed as colonnades, aisled halls, or outlets around courtyards. The *macellum* sold mostly provisions, especially fruits and vegetables, and could be found alongside the forum and basilica. Examples are known at Leicester, Wroxeter and Verulamium. Shops usually fronted on to the crowded, noisy and smelly main streets in the centres of towns with the dwelling premises of the owners and tenants alongside or above. York's Bootham – 'the place of the booths' – was known as Macellum.

The public bath house

One constituent of a forum, the public bath house, has been found at the north-east end of York's Micklegate. The walls were a huge 2.2 metres thick and up to 3.5 metres high. A water pipe found at Wellington Row and a fountain at Bishophill are evidence of the piped water supply to such bath houses and the *mansiones*. The bath house evidence comprises a heated room on a site in Church Street and part of a *caldarium* (hot steam room with plunge bath), under-floor heating ducts and a cold plunge bath which can be seen in the Roman Bath Museum under the Roman Bath public house in St Sampson's Square.

Other structures to be found in or near the forum include theatres (only four known in Britannia at Verulamium, Canterbury, Colchester, and possibly at Brough-on-Humber); amphitheatres (seven are so far confirmed by archaeological remains: London, Caistor-by-Norwich, Carmarthen,

Dorchester, Silchester, Chichester, Cirencester. The one at Silchester probably held around 3,000 people; and triumphal arches (as at Camulodunum) although there is no evidence that York ever had such an arch.

Altars and temples

Roman Britain offers a wide variety of shrines and temples to a range of deities and cults. Examples from York include: an inscription to a temple of Serapis-Osiris and an altar to Mother Goddesses of the household by Gaius Julius Crescens found in Nunnery Lane.

The Crescens altar is dedicated to the Mother Goddesses of the household (*RIB* 652) is of limestone with a damaged capital; sides fluted, back plain. Found in St Mary's Convent in 1880; now in the Yorkshire Museum: YORYM: 2001.12520. The dedication reads:

> G(aius) Iuliu(s)
> Crescens
> Matri-
> bus Do-
> mesticis
> v(otum) s(olvit) m(erito) l(ibens)

Image courtesy of and © York Museums Trust

Gaius Julius Crescens, to the Mother Goddesses of the household, willingly and deservedly fulfils his vow.

Described in Charles Wellbeloved's *Eboracum* as 'Altar, of soft magnesian limestone, 8in by 17 and 1/2ins by 6 and 1/2 ins, elegantly carved. The sides are fluted and have been coated with gesso and painted, the flutings yellow and their stops red … The top is damaged but the altar is otherwise in excellent condition. The Matres were a popular Celtic triad of goddesses.' Found with two other altars and the statue of Mars (YORYM: 1998.26).

Another Crescens was remembered on (*RIB*) 671 on a tombstone excavated during extension work at the Mount School in 1911; it is still there. The inscription ran:

> D(is) M(anibus)
> L(ucius) Bebius
> Aug(usta) Cres-
> cens Vin(delicum)
> mil(es) leg(ionis) VI
> Vic(tricis) P(iae) F(idelis)
> an(norum) XLIII
> stip(endiorum) XXIII
>
> h(anc) a(ram) f(aciendum) c(uravit)

To the spirits of the departed: Lucius Bebius Crescens, of Augusta Vindelicum, soldier of the Sixth Legion Pia Fidelis, aged 43, of 23 years' service; his heir took care to build this altar.

The Egyptian cult of Serapis was a particular favourite of Severus; the temple was erected and financed by the legionary commander of the VIth, Claudius Hieronymianus, around AD 200; its dedication stone was uncovered in Toft Green. Hieronymianus may well have served in Egypt which is probably where he will have come into contact with Serapis; he went on to become governor of Capadoccia and is mentioned in Tertullian's *Address to Scapula Tertullus*: angry at his wife's conversion to Christianity, Hieronymianus brought 'much ill to the Christians' there. Hieronymianus is also identified with the senator mentioned in Ulpian *Digest* 33, 7, 12, 40. His own pagan leanings are, of course, expressed in the dedication stone in which he is named as the benefactor of the re-built Roman temple dedicated to Serapis.

The Serapis dedication-slab (*RIB* 658) was found in 1770 and is now in the Yorkshire Museum: YORYM 1998.27. It reads

> Deo sancto
> Serapi
> templum a so-
> lo fecit Cl(audius) Hierony-
> mianus leg(atus)
> leg(ionis) VI Vic(tricis)

To the holy god Serapis Claudius Hieronymianus, legate of the VIth Legion Victrix, built this temple from the ground up.

In terms of religion, Eboracum was decidedly cosmopolitan. The Romans brought with them their polytheistic religion and their complicated, incestuous pantheon, as well as other faiths adopted, adapted and syncretised over many years of foreign conquest and civilising. The Roman soldiers, the camp followers and the city that grew up around the military fortress signified, with their various deities and the temples which honoured and housed them, the first recorded religious presence in what was to become York.

The Romans had gods and goddesses for every conceivable stage and facet of life, and death – from conception to life in the afterlife. Deities and *numen*, spirits, attended the Romans' every act and were worshipped accordingly. Excavations have revealed the altars and dedication stones dedicated to thirty or so different divinities set up at one time or another, including Venus, Mars; Mercury; Bellona (goddess of war); Neptune; Hercules; Jupiter, Tethys, Hospitality and the Home (*Jupiter, Hospitalis et Penates*); Britannia, Veteris, Silvanus, Toutatis, Chnoubis and Fortune,

The Serapis temple inscription. Image courtesy of and © York Museums Trust

the Divinity of the Emperor (*numen Augusti*) as well as references to the spiritual representation (*genius Eboraci*) of Eboracum, the spirit of the place (*Genius Loci*) and dedications to the Mother Goddess and various local and regional deities. Celtic deities include Boudiga, Arciaco, and Sucelus – the latter two unique to Eboracum in Britannia. The surviving remains of the temple of Hercules gives us two of the names of the men who rebuilt it: Titus Perpetuus and Aeternus – citizens of York both.

Aelius Spartianus was a historian who wrote the biographies of Hadrian, Didius Julianus, Severus, Niger, Caracalla and Geta for the notoriously unreliable *Historia Augusta* – a late Roman collection of biographies of the Roman emperors, their junior colleagues, designated heirs and usurpers of the period 117 to 284. It was written during the reigns of Diocletian and Constantine I. William Combe in *The History and Antiquities of the City of York* (1785) and referenced by Drake in *Eboracum* (1788) suggests that Spartianus reports that a temple to Bellona existed just outside Micklegate Bar in the context of Severus' return from Scotland in AD 221. The emperor visited the shrine to perform a sacrifice in thanks for his victories but the soothsayer on duty (an 'ignorant Augur') supplied black instead of white animals. Severus was appalled and returned to his palace in York while, adding insult to injury, the black beasts were carelessly allowed to follow close behind to the very doors of the palace. A bad and unpropitious day for the emperor – he died soon after.

The more exotic and personal worship of eastern deities is much in evidence including Atys and Serapis: the cult of Mithras, always popular with the military, features on a sculpture showing Mithras characteristically slaying a bull and in a dedication to Arimanius, the god of evil in the Mithraism tradition. The Mithraic relief found in 1747 near St Martin-cum-Gregory church in Micklegate could suggest the existence of a temple to Mithras in the centre of the *colonia*.

When the VIth Legion arrived in York in or around 120 they brought with them that inveterate traveller, the emperor Hadrian, who had made the decisive decision to plug his increasingly porous final frontier by building what we know now as Hadrian's Wall. York, as stated, would have been a vital staging post on the way to the wall for troops, construction workers (mostly legionary soldiers), the matériel supply chain and logistics generally.

As we have seen, by the years 211–5 during the reign of Caracalla, York's status was elevated further to capital of Lower Britain (Britannia inferior) when Britannia was divided into two provinces. For Severus see Sextus Aurelius Victor (*c*.AD 320–*c*.90) the author of a short history of imperial Rome, entitled *De Caesaribus* covering the period from Augustus to Constantius II.

York was by now the largest and most important civilian place in the north with a sizeable population. In 237 York was promoted to *colonia* status (by Caracalla as Colonia Eboracensium), the highest rank of Roman city. In common with typical *colonia* practice throughout the empire, veterans from the IXth legion would have been granted land next to the fortress on which they would have run businesses sourcing supplies such as stone and timber as well as for grazing and arable agriculture. Near the banks of the Ouse in Coney Street archaeologists have revealed the remains of two first- to early second-century grain warehouses not far from the legionary pottery and tile kilns on the approach road to the fortress.

The levels of Roman cities are: *colonia*; *municipium*; *civitas* capitals and *vicus*.

Where there are mosaics there would have been money. We have evidence from the late third to early fourth century of town houses which were completed with mosaic pavements: at St Mary, Castlegate and in Aldwark, Bar Lane, Toft Green and Clementhorpe. Particularly impressive is the extensive town house in Bishophill built in the late third century; it can boast at least two ranges of rooms around a central courtyard. The later Roman York witnessed some rebuilding including the so-called 'Anglian Tower', about 60 metres from the Multangular Tower.

The strategic importance of York: roads and rivers

Rivers and roads were key factors in many aspects of the Roman occupation. As with any occupying army, the Romans had to move supplies and they had to trade. They also needed to move large numbers of troops and their matériel from place to place, often at short notice and in emergency situations. The Romans maintained, as we know, four legions in Britain, in total about 20,000 soldiers supported by a further 20,000 auxiliaries, so deploying a full legion would on average entail moving around 5,000 men, their carts, mules and horses, equipment and supplies, and the extensive baggage train.

An efficient road system and supply chain was therefore required to support all of these needs. No doubt this volume of people and their encumbrances in some areas would clog up and damage trackways, bridges and fords, making them difficult to use, often causing the column to be strung out and therefore vulnerable to attack. The ordinary Roman soldier carried all of his kit and weapons with him. This is where the Roman road comes in and, while not all road building was driven by military considerations and stretches of road were built to service farms, villas and other places with no military significance, the Roman army had to be able to move from A to B in the most expeditious way possible. It was not until the German Bundesautobahn network was initiated in the 1930s that anything like a comparable road scheme was completed; unlike in the Roman empire, the military value to the Germans was limited as all major military transports in Germany were made by train to save fuel.

Wade's Causeway: a stretch of 'Romanised' Roman road at Goathland on the North York Moors north of York. It is a 1.2 mile-long section (1.9 km) on the eastern edge of Wheeldale Moor, facing Howl Moor. It runs in an approximately north-north-easterly direction between grid reference SE 80344 97382 and grid reference SE 81077 98697

Moreover, not every road we call a Roman road was in fact a Roman road. It is likely that as well as developing parts of the road network from scratch, there was also a programme of selective improvements. Existing pre-Roman unpaved (and inefficient) trackways that were to form major supply routes or used for moving large numbers would have been upgraded. Wade's Causeway (named after a local giant) is an example of this: until recently it was assumed to be of Roman origin (Ivan Margary *Roman Roads In Britain* (1957) catalogue #81b) but it is actually a winding, linear monument of approximately 6,000 years old. The thinking was that it was probably constructed to connect the Roman Cawthorne Camp to the south with the Roman garrison fort at Lease Rigg near Grosmont to the north.

In almost four centuries of occupation the Romans built about 2,000 miles of roads in Britain with the aim of connecting key locations by the most direct possible route. The roads were all paved and all-season and all-weather, to permit heavy freight-wagons to be used the year round, whatever the weather.

Before the Romans came Britain had few, if any, substantial bridges, so all rivers and streams would have been crossed by fords. Even well after the Romans had come and gone, many towns were at fording points, and the point nearest to the sea that a river could be forded was a major consideration in most journeys and military manoeuvres. In York the Ouse was bridged.

The Roman army was multi-skilled, with people who could quickly and efficiently construct bridges, plan and organise the building of defensive forts, signal stations and other structures in wood and stone; they could build boats; indeed, their skill sets were not so dissimilar to the mechanical engineering function of the REME in the modern British army. Ordinary soldiers were expected to build walls and fortresses as required, competent as they were at quarrying, cutting and shifting stone. Apart from military facilities, many villas and towns were built by the soldiery.

York then ticked all the strategic boxes; it was sited at the confluence of the Ouse and the Foss, some 50 miles from the sea. The site was on an elevated moraine some 10.5 metres above sea level and high enough above the local water table to avoid flooding. The roads we know of include:

Dere Street leading north-west from the city north through Clifton towards the site of Cataractonium (modern Catterick)

Cade's Road west towards Petuaria (modern Brough)

Ermine Street south towards Lindum (modern Lincoln).

A road bypassing the south wall of the fortress, between the fortress and the Ouse has not been formally tracked, although its path is thought to run beneath Museum Gardens. Other roads came in to York from Malton and Stamford Bridge; in all eleven roads are known to converge on the city, full details of which can be found at www.british-history.ac.uk/rchme/york/vol1/.

The initial road network was, of course, built by the army to facilitate military communications. The emphasis was on linking up army bases, rather than anything else. To that end, three important cross-routes were established connecting the major legionary bases by AD 80 as the frontier of the Roman-occupied zone advanced:

Roman Britain about AD 150, showing the main roads

Exeter (Isca)–Lincoln (Lindum)

Gloucester (Glevum)–York (Eboracum)

Caerleon (Isca)–York via Wroxeter (Viroconium) and Chester (Deva)

Augustus formalised all routes of official communication when he established the *cursus publicus* (literally, the *public way*), a state-run courier and logistics service. Apart from acting as a means for distributing the general post the *cursus* gave the legions the tactical opportunity to summon reinforcements and issue status reports before any situation got out of hand. Slaves were also sent through the system. The roads leading into and out of Eboracum would have formed an integral part not just the road network in Britannia but of the empire-wide *cursus publicus*.

Essentially, it was made up of thousands of posting stations (*mutationes* or *mansiones*) along the major road systems of the empire where horses were watered, shoed, cared for by vets, stabled, and passed over to dispatch riders (initially imperial *tabellarii* but later soldiers as the system became militarised). In 1969 the carved base of what was probably a milestone was found in the forecourt of the Eboracum *principia*.

The Romans have dictated the layout of the present city. As we have seen, two of York's main streets, Stonegate and Petergate, roughly follow the line of the two principal streets in the fortress, the *via praetoria* and the *via principalis* respectively. The *via praetoria* led to the great south-west gate (*porta praetorian*) where St Helen's Square is now, revealing that the fortress faced south-west towards the River Ouse.

The Romans put their rivers to good use: shiploads of goods would have come in on the Ouse via the Humber from the North Sea some fifty miles to the east, and on the Foss; two possible wharves on the east bank of the River Foss support this idea. The Ouse was navigable from the North Sea, which facilitated the transport of troops and support staff and the delivery of military supplies and equipment. A large deposit of grain, found in a timber-structure beneath modern day Coney Street, on the north bank of the Ouse points to storehouses for moving goods via the river.

The Garrison

The legion

The word legion derives from the Latin *legio*, meaning a selection, a levy of troops, a legion. We know that four legions were part of the initial invasion force in AD 43 – some 20,000–25,000 troops. A legion, numbering approximately 5,000 men, consisted of ten cohorts; a cohort was 480 men made up of six centuries, and each century of 80 men plus approximately 20 orderlies to make up the 'century', was commanded by a centurion. The basic unit was a *contubernium* – eight men who shared a tent when on campaign and a barrack room when in the fortress; ten *contubernia* made a century. The legionary troops comprised mostly infantry but a cavalry unit was also attached.

Legionaries were Roman citizens with all the benefits and privileges that conferred. The soldiers, if they weren't killed or severely disabled, were required to serve for 25 years before retirement as a veteran. A long time, but worth waiting for as veteran status, apart from a worthwhile gratuity, bought land in the *colonia* and land unlocked the door to political and social advancement. Detachments of auxiliary troops were key to the legions – just like reservists in today's British army; these were recruited from the indigenous populations of the various provinces of the Roman empire and included special forces such as archers or marine commandos who excelled in swimming with full armour, literally armed to the teeth. Auxiliaries were not Roman citizens; they were enlisted to fight in suport in cohorts or *alae* (wings) of 500 men or so. After 25 years they retired and were granted Roman citizenship, as were their dependants.

The commanding officer, the *legatus legionis*, was always of senatorial rank, in his thirties serving a three to four year posting as part of his *cursus honorum*, a career path taking in pre-ordained military and administrative posts culminating in the consulship. The 2 IC (*tribunus laticlavus*, second in command) would also be of senatorial rank and in his early twenties. There were usually five other senior officers: *tribuni augusticlavii* who were equestrians (one down from a senator) and who served for three years. The most important was the camp prefect, *praefectus castrorum*, who looked after the camp, training and equipment.

The demographics of the Roman army changed significantly between the first and second centuries AD. In the first half of the first century 65 per cent of the military were from Italy; this had diminished to less than 1 per cent by the second century, so the soldiers in York will have been a very diverse group. This is reflected on a number of headstones and altars. At the same time we can estimate that the empire-wide Roman army numbered 155,000 legionaries and 218,000 auxiliaries.

The IXth Hispana – Legio Nona Hispana

Badged after its earlier successes in Iberia, the legion arrived in Britain in AD 43 from Pannonia (around present-day western Hungary and eastern Austria) after the disastrous Battle of the Teutoburg Forest in AD 9. In AD 50, the IXth was one of two legions that defeated Caratacus at Caer Caradoc. Around the same time, the legion built the fort, Lindum Colonia, at Lincoln. Under the command of Caesius Nasica they put down the first revolt of Venutius between 52 and 57. The Spanish connection comes from their service in Hispania in the lengthy campaign against the Cantabrians (25–13 BC). The nickname 'Hispana' is first found during the reign of Augustus and probably originated at that time.

The IXth suffered a serious reverse at the Battle of Camulodunum under Quintus Petillius Cerialis during the AD 60 rebellion of Boudica

The eagle of the IXth – Image courtesy of and © York Museums Trust

when most of the infantry were killed in a disastrous attempt to relieve Camulodunum (Colchester). Only the cavalry escaped. The legion was later reinforced with legionaries from Germania. When Cerialis returned as governor of Britain ten years later, he took command of the IXth again in a successful campaign against the Brigantes in 71–2, to subdue north-central Britain. Around this time they constructed the new fortress at Eboracum; the legion was part of Agricola's invasion force in Caledonia in 82–3.

The IXth was last heard of in Eboracum AD 108 as recorded in an inscribed stone tablet discovered in 1864 – the memorial to Lucius Duccius Rufinus, a standard bearer of the IXth. They transferred to Nijmegen (Noviomagus Batavorum) in Hadrian's reign and then to the east of the empire. Disaster struck at some point and the legion was disbanded by AD 165.

Rosemary Sutcliff's 1954 *The Eagle of the Ninth*, tells of a young Roman officer, Marcus Flavius Aquila, trying to recover the eagle standard of his father's legion beyond Hadrian's Wall.

The VIth Victrix – Legio Sexta Victrix

The VIth arrived in Britain around AD 122 from Xanten after a posting at Neuss – both on the Rhine. It was the soldiers from the VIth who built much of Hadrian's Wall; the legion stayed until the withdrawal of all Roman troops in 410. The legionary badge was a bull which was adopted in the insignia of the province of Lower Britain.

'Victorious Sixth Legion' was founded in 41 BC by Octavian, later Augustus (as the twin legion of VI Ferrata (iron clad); it first saw action in Perusia in 41 BC during the civil wars; served against Sextus Pompeius, and in 31 BC fought in the Battle of Actium with Octavian against Mark Antony.

The legion took part in the final stage of the Roman conquest of Hispania, like the IXth, participating in Augustus' major war against the Cantabrians that finally brought Iberia under Roman rule. The legion stayed in Spain for nearly a century and adopted the *cognomen* 'Hispaniensis', founding the city of Legio (modern-day León). The cognomen *Victrix* (Victorious) dates back to the reign of Nero. But Nero was unpopular in the area, and when the governor of Hispania Tarraconensis, Servius Sulpicius Galba, declared his wish to overthrow Nero, the legion supported him and Galba was proclaimed emperor in the VI *Victrix* legionary camp.

In 119, Hadrian relocated the legion to northern Britannia where it was instrumental in securing victory; the legion would eventually replace the diminished IX *Hispana* at Eboracum. Having helped in the construction of Hadrian's Wall the VIth assisted in building the Antonine Wall. Legio VI was awarded the honorary title '*Britannica*' by Commodus in AD 184 following his own adoption of the title.

What did all those legionaries do all day and night?

Obviously, a lot of the time was spent away from the fortress in combat, subduing fractious tribes, building forts and walls to keep insurgents at bay. When in the fortress we can estimate that the legionary did a lot of guard duty. In a unit of 800 men 20 per cent were on guard once every 24 hours, so 160 men every day. In a full legion, then, 1,200 men out of 6,000 would have been on guard every day. Patrols, parades, combat training, cooking, admin, maintenance and cleaning of weapons and armour occupied much of the rest of the time, as in any army.

Attaining full complement must have been problematic with absenteeism caused by extra-mural exercises, secondments, and illness. One of the Vindolanda tablets (# 154) records where in one instance of 752 men on the roll, only 265 were actually available for duties.

The civilian settlement (*vicus* or *canaba*)

The fortress was strictly military. So what about the commercial, cultural, spiritual and social needs of the fortress soldiery when they were having a spot of rest and recuperation? On the other side of the fortress wall civilians from near and far were eager to take advantage of the extensive commercial opportunites brought by the garrison of more than 5,000 men, be they selling bread, arena tickets (*panem et circenses*) or their bodies. The fort was a magnet drawing in artisans, labourers, traders, wives, actors, dancers, musicians, slaves, camp followers and prostitutes. Roman soldiers were not officially permitted to marry although many undoubtedly did form relationships with local women.

A *vicus* could and often did, over the years, flourish and grow until it attained the status of an independent *municipium* in its own right; it may then even graduate to *colonia* status, as is the case with Eboracum. Here the ever burgeoning civilian settlement followed the line of some of the roads leading in and out the fortress, for example at the southwest gate where the road crossed the Ouse Bridge, then on up the hill to enter the walls near Micklegate Bar. There is *vicus* evidence also on the north-east side of the river around Spurriergate and Nessgate. A replica of the dedication stone from a temple of Hercules is set into the wall of a building in Nessgate where the original was found; wharves have been discovered along the Foss which may have been a harbour, and a mosaic has been unearthed south of the fortress east angle. Burials have been excavated along a road along the line of Toft Green and Tanner Row; around AD 200 there was a bronze workshop at Bishophill, later replaced by two stone buildings. Clementhorpe is the site of a grand house typical of those which came complete with under-floor heating, some mosaics and frescoed walls.

Excavations of the Foss wharves mentioned above have yielded up the stone base of a tower crane; the harbour here would have served the *vicus* trade while the fortress would have been self-sufficient with its own river craft and pilots, one of whom was M. Minucius Audens of the VIth legion who dedicated an altar which is now in the Yorkshire Museum. Audens (his name means brave and bold) dedicated the altar to the Mother Goddess of Africa, Italy and Gaul. M. Aurelius Lunaris would also have been a regular visitor at the wharves as a commercial contractor shipping wine and olive oil from to York from Bordeaux around 237; he was a *sevir Augustalis* at York and Lincoln; his altar in Bordeaux describes him as *ab Eboraci avectus* – 'having sailed away from York'. M. Verecundius Diogenes would have been there too – according to the inscription on his coffin a *moritex* or shipper – he hailed from Bourges and settled with his wife, Julia Fortunata, to a comfortable life in York.

Other cargoes bound for York included samian ware and fine glassware. Bordeaux was an important trading link with York, as indeed was the Rhine estuary where the merchant L. Viducius Placidus from Rouen plied his trade. His dedication stone to Nehalennia – a goddess with a responsibility for ensuring the safety of cargoes – was dredged up from the Rhine estuary in 1970. York Archaeological Trust, during their Clementhorpe excavations in 1976, found it again, over-inscribed with a new dedication, this time from AD 221 to the spirit of the place and the divinities of the emperors.

The Ouse also had a domestic function: millstone grit came in via the river Aire and Tadcaster limestone via the Wharfe. Products from the Nene Valley kilns (tableware which took over from Samian in the third century) probably arrived by way of the Trent and Ouse and then the Car and Foss Dikes. Corn, gypsum, lead and coal will have arrived by road or barge.

In 1860 the grounds of the manor house at Dringhouses gave up a fine tomb relief (now in the Yorkshire Museum) showing a smith complete with protective leather apron, hammer and tongs. Bronze pins and wrought iron were worked in a workshop found in Bishophill Senior from the second century. Other craftsmen at work in York included stonemasons and carvers of jet and bone.

Food

Unsurprisingly, given the sheer size of the settlement at York – fortress and *vicus*, food and its provision were hugely important. Archaeological evidence tells us much about food consumption and diet locally with significant evidence for cereal crops and animal husbandry. As noted, a first-century warehouse fire in Coney Street in the *vicus* revealed from the charred grain that spelt wheat and barley were the most common cereal grains at that time. The fire was in fact, at the second warehouse which stood on the site of the first; its predecessor was demolished, it seems, after a massive infestation attested by well-preserved grain beetles; the building was sealed with clay before a replacement was constructed.

Cattle, sheep, goat and pig were the major sources of meat but beef was by far the most popular. Animal bones found at 9 Blake Street indicate that the residents were partial to smoked or salted beef. The bones of (an edible) dormouse (*glis glis*) have been found amongst the Roman rubbish – stuffed dormice were a delicacy. There is also evidence that fish and crabs were on the menu: the crabs probably came from the Bridlington area and herring from the Humber estuary.

Romano-British 'hunt cups' depict hunting scenes; *mortaria* (hemispherical or conical bowls, with coarse sand or grit embedded into the internal surface) have been excavated in the city and large millstones have been found in rural sites outside the *colonia* at Heslington and Stamford Bridge.

Funeral feasts are depicted on the tombstones of Julia Velva, Mantinia Maercia and Aelia Aeliana to cater for their culinary needs in the afterlife; Julia's family is shown reclining on a couch and being served food and wine. Julia Velva is depicted holding a wine jar with her daughter, the wife of Aurelius Mercurialis, who can be seen holding a scroll – possibly Julia's

Julia Velva's tomb and inscription (*RIB* 688). Image courtesy of and © York Museums Trust

will. She lived a good life – 50 years – and was believed by the family to participate in the annual celebration, as a shade.

RIB describes it as follows:

> The deceased, Julia Velva, reclines on a couch, though appearing to stand behind it, with a cup in her hand. At the head, in front of a second table, stands her heir Mercurialis, who is bearded and wears tunic, cloak, and boots and holds in his right hand the scroll of the will. On the left of a second three-legged table (in front of Julia's couch) sits a lady in a wicker chair with a bird in her hands. On the right of the table stands a second figure with a jug, presumably an attendant. The formula suis, 'family', suggests that the figure in the chair is a relative of Mercurialis.

Several inhumation burials from Trentholme Drive contained hen's eggs placed in ceramic urns as essential grave goods for the deceased.

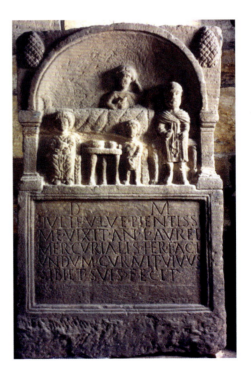

Relief with Julia Velva on couch with young girl, boy servant and Aurelius Mercurialis above inscription. Julia Velva, whose head, with hair parted in the middle is reclining on a couch and propping her head on her left arm, which rests on a cushion. She holds a wine jar in her right hand. In front of the couch, left to right, are shown a young girl seated on a basket chair and clasping a pet bird, a three-legged table on which are dishes of food, a boy standing with his right hand on the table and holding a jug in his left, while Aurelius Mercurialis, bearded, holds a scroll in his right hand. Found in 1922, during construction of Albermarle Road, near The Mount. Courtesy of York Museums Trust.

Burials and the headless gladiators

The Roman presence in York lasted for over 300 years; thousands of Romans were born here during that time, and thousands died here, and were buried. What do we know about how and where the inhabitants of Eboracum dealt with and disposed of their dead?

Roman law prohibited burials inside inhabited areas, mostly on the grounds of religion and hygiene, but space too was a factor – Roman towns were intensely crowded and there was simply no room for the luxury of an intra-mural cemetery. Only the imperial family (in the empire) and the Vestal Virgins were exempt. Cremations on funeral pyres would also have posed a serious urban fire hazard.

The sheer importance of this ruling is underlined by the fact that it was one of the twelve laws enshrined in the august and ancient 'The Law of the Twelve Tables' (*Leges Duodecim Tabularum* or *Duodecim Tabulae*) of about 450 BC – legislation that formed the very foundation of Roman law. Table Ten tells us that a 'dead person shall not be buried or burnt in the City'.

It was, therefore, usual practice for interments to take place alongside the principal roads into and out of a fortress, outside the walls. Over the centuries as today, York was expanding beyond the medieval city walls. We have uncovered much evidence of Roman burials – occasionally as single burials but more usually in extensive cemeteries of single- and multiple-occupation graves. The discoveries have shown us that burial practices varied greatly over both time and according to the social or military status of the deceased. Fashions too changed: in some periods we have mostly cremations, at other times burials predominate: until the late second century, cremation was the preferred exit from this life and co-existed with burials for some 70 years. Then burials became the method of despatch of choice with cremation discontinued from about 270. As we have noted, the emperor Septimius Severus himself was cremated after his death in York in 211 before his remains were returned to Rome.

Trentholme Drive has yielded 40 cinerary urns and part of the *ustrina* – the place where the dead were incinerated. Unsurprisingly, the charred debris found here contained human and animal bones, nails (from boots, coffins and biers), pottery sherds, rings, pins and brooches. Local wood and coal from Middleton Main and Middleton Little seams near Leeds have been discovered.

In York calcined bones have been unearthed in urns and amphorae; a glass jar with a lead bung in the neck found in 1861 contained the ashes of Corellia Optata, a 13-year-old girl whose movingly inscribed tombstone was set up by her grieving father, Quintus Corellius Fortis. Then there are three lead canisters – one of which bore the sad inscription 'to Ulpia Felicissima, who lived for 8 years 11 months and ? days, Marcus Ulpius Felix and ? Andronica, her parents had this made'. A number of stone coffins or cists have also been found, mainly on the railway station site with another two in the Multangular Tower. Famously there is also a tiled tomb made from eight *tegulae* or flat tiles each with the stamp of Legio IX *Hispana*.

Cemeteries at Burton Stone Lane and Clifton Fields are half a mile from the fortress with others at Heworth, Dringhouses, the Mount (including Trentholme Drive), Holgate, at the Railway Station, Nunnery Lane – Bar Convent, Baile Hill, Clementhorpe, Clifford's Tower, Hawthorne Drive, Heworth Green, Bootham near St Peter's School, near what was Queen Anne's Grammar School in Clifton where St Olave's School is now, Burton Stone Lane, Clifton Fields, and Fishergate. There was a small inhumation cemetery near the junction of Haxby and Wigginton Roads comprising twelve burials; it yielded pottery on its discovery in 1833 – all of these, of course, were outside the fortress walls.

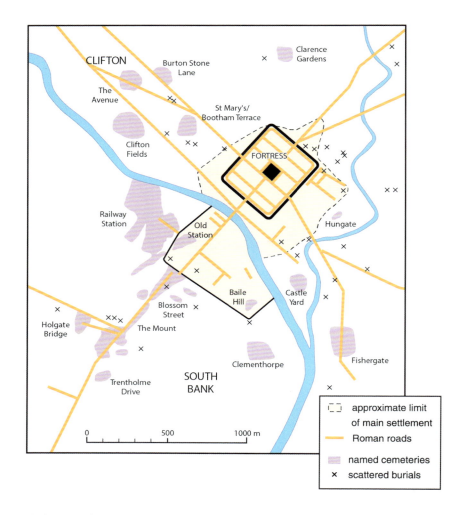

The location of burial sites along the roads of Eboracum. Courtesy and © York Archaeological Trust

Wooden coffins (subject, of course, as they were to decomposition) were the norm, but York is unusual in the large number of stone (90) and lead (25) coffins found. Women (or at least the wealthier women) were often buried adorned with their jewellery and the finest jet items from around Whitby – bracelets, rings, hair pins, medallions with figures in relief – have been found in York burials. Burials vary from cremated remains either in ceramic pots or holes in the ground to the more common inhumations, and, again for the wealthy or high ranking military and civic leaders, inscribed sarcophagi sometimes, but rarely, placed in elaborate purpose-built mausoleums. A vaulted tomb discovered in 1807 still survives in the cellar at 104 The Mount. Made from brick and stone it is 3 metres x 2 metres, 2.5 metres high and contains the bones of a woman aged about 40; her finger bones revealed that she had never been troubled by manual work of any nature. Two lachrymatories, glass phials, were found on either side of her skull.

York, then, has one of the largest collections of stone coffins in Britain. Weighing between 1.5 and 2 tonnes they are made from millstone grit quarried in the Pennines. Fine examples of sarcophagi are in the Yorkshire Museum together with tombstone grave markers erected in remembrance of Eboracum's more prominent citizens.

Twenty-five lead coffins have been excavated here – some lined with wood, some enclosed in wood, one as the lining to a stone coffin – this was discovered in 1875 under the railway station booking office and

The tomb

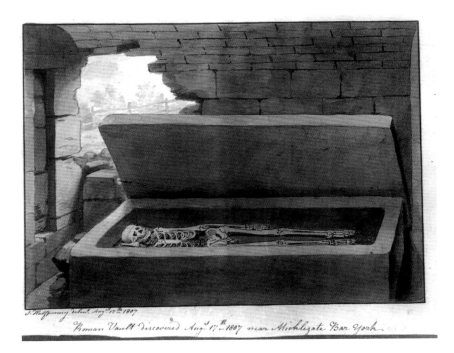

contained the skeleton of a teenage girl whose auburn hair tied in a bun with two jet pins is now resplendent in the Yorkshire Museum. A stone cist was found in 1952 in Trentholme Drive with the remains of a 40-year-old man in a wooden coffin: an urn had been deliberately placed under the coffin, directly beneath the heart of the deceased.

Between 1951 and 1958 a 240 sq.m area around Trentholme Drive was excavated yielding the skeletons of over 300 men women and children. Two iron arrow heads and an iron shield boss were found but apart from these military objects the cemetery was civilian. Grave goods indicated the dead to have been relatively poor. The burials were haphazard with no placement planning in evidence; indeed the cemetery had been used a number of times with subsequent burials overlying earlier occupants and with bones all over the place.

Most of the graves were accompanied by a pot or pots containing food and drink to facilitate the deceased's journey through the underworld into the after life. 150 complete or near complete pots were found in all positions in relation to the bodies. Organised laying-out of bodies was absent with every imaginable position represented: five were buried on their faces, some (usually children) were crouched, others on their sides, two were back-to-back and foot-to-foot, two teenagers were embracing each other; two were folded up in a sack and had been dumped in a hole. Most, of course, were on their backs, arms at their side or folded across their chests, legs crossed or straight. 2,500 nails indicated the presence of coffins. Animal and bird bones suggest they were buried with the dead – another source of post-mortem food; animals included sheep, goats, oxen, horse, cats, pigs and deer. The embracing youths referred to above were found with the complete skeleton of a hen on the uppermost's back. Three of the pots had coins in them, four contained hen's eggshells. Seven skulls contained the obligatory coin to pay surly Charon the fare required for crossing the River Styx.

The excavations here did much to advance our knowledge of Roman life: over 75 per cent of the people died before age 40 – only 65 out of 342 reached beyond 45. The tallest man was 6'4", the average 5'5"; women averaged 5'2" – slightly smaller than today's average. Rheumatism and arthritis were present in everyone over 30 – a consequence of the damp and cold. Skeletal evidence shows many of the inhabitants to have lived a life of conflict – not especially surprising given the Romans' endless warring and the lengthy military careers of its soldiery. Twenty-one healed upper and lower limb fractures have been found including fractured thigh bones; several more thigh bones displayed depressions consistent with sword cuts. Squatting facets – the remodelling of the bones at the front of the *talus*, or ankle – in women's bones indicate that they spent a lot of time squatting: cooking and tending the fires. Dental health was generally good although there were signs of extractions, abcesses and decay; largely free from caries, less than 5 per cent of the 5,000 teeth examined showed signs of decay. Grit lined mortaria and stone querns no doubt contributed to the well-worn condition of the teeth, as well as plenty of roughage in the diet.

Female skulls showed the women to be almost all of Celtic origin but the men were a more varied group: five came from the eastern Mediterranean, seven were Scandinavian while one was negro; there were also a number of Germans.

Gypsum burials

The cemetery beneath the railway station was particularly fruitful after excavations in 1839–41, 1845, and 1870–7. A number of sarcophagi were unearthed including those of Flavius Bellator and Julia Fortunata. Inhumation burial in sarcophagi often entails encasing the body in gypsum and then in a lead coffin. The gypsum casts, when found undisturbed, often retain a cast impression of the deceased in a textile shroud – the numerous sarcophagi from Eboracum have provided a large number of these casts, in some cases with cloth surviving stuck to the gypsum.

Two gypsum burials at York have revealed evidence of frankincense and another for Pistacia (a genus of flowering plants in the cashew family) resin used in funerary rites. This is the northernmost confirmed use of aromatic resins in mortuary contexts during the Roman period.

A gypsum burial on display in the Yorkshire Museum. Image courtesy of and © Yorkshire Museums Trust

Gypsum (hydrous calcium chlorate) has been found in some of the sarcophagi encasing the body of the deceased – no doubt an attempt to embalm and preserve; unfortunately gypsum acts in the opposite way – as an accelerant to decomposition of bones and tissue. Nevertheless, the gypsum does leave a trace of the body outline and winding sheet – the most interesting example is the outline of a woman with the outline of a newborn between her legs; casualties no doubt of childbirth mortality. The burial is described in *Eboracum* as:

> Large coffin, of stone, found in July 1851, at a depth of 3ft under a house at the corner of Price's Lane and Bishopgate Street, containing the skeleton of a woman with the skeleton of a child between her legs. The bodies had been covered in gypsum, forming a cast … with fragments of cloth still adhering to it. No grave goods are preserved from this

coffin, but a hole above the left shoulder of the woman's skeleton shows whence some were removed."

Not surprisingly, ingesting gypsum is not good for you, as Caius Proculeius, a good friend of the emperor Augustus found out to his cost. A matter-of-fact Pliny the Elder (*Natural History* 36, 59) tells us how, 'suffering from violent pains in the stomach, [he] swallowed gypsum, and so put an end to his existence'.

In April 2018 seventy-five Roman skeletons were discovered on the site of the former Newington Hotel in Mount Vale Drive; they were unearthed under the swimming pool, in an extension to the Roman burial ground further up Mount Vale. York Archaeological Trust describes it as follows:

> Included among exciting finds have been grave goods in the form of pottery, dishes, jars, flagons and beakers and also traces of the coffins in which the dead were laid to rest. Notably very little in the way of personal adornment has been found, only a single jet pin and the badly corroded copper alloy remains of what may have been part of a head or hair band. These burials are currently thought to date to a period spanning the second to fourth centuries AD and, as the finds suggest, to have been of people of a relatively lowly social status.

Driffield Terrace and the headless gladiators

Possible evidence for gladiators keeps emerging in Eboracum. An excavation before building work underneath the Yorkshire Museum in 2009 located a male skeleton for which osteoarchaeological investigation led to suggestions that he may have died as a gladiator in Eboracum.

Trentholm Drive 'is part of an extensive funerary landscape known to line the southern approach road to Eboracum stretching over the course of a mile or more' (https://www.yorkarchaeology.co.uk/secondmentsblogsdfsdfsdf/2019/5/31/the-newington-hotel-site-and-gladiators-a-cemetery-of-secrets)

There has been much publicity surrounding ninety-six burials found in part of the sprawling extra-mural Roman cemetery around the Mount and in Driffield Terrace in particular (SE59324510 and SE59285095). Evidence is pointing to the conclusion that these were gladiators who had been decapitated, as described on the web page above.

The burials took place during the second and third centuries AD, maybe into the fourth.

York Archaeological Trust has been at the forefront of research relating to these excavations along with partners at various universities:

'A Cemetery of Secrets'

From 2004 to 2005 we excavated eighty burials at Driffield Terrace in York … The burials displayed evidence that so intrigued the archaeologists that further investigation was needed. The male skeletons displayed deliberate trauma, interesting pathology and peri-mortem decapitation. Working with York, Durham, Reading and Trinity College Dublin Universities we have been continuing our search for the answer to the question of whether these people could have been a group of gladiators, who lived and fought in York during the Roman occupation.

Scientific work that has been carried out by experts includes genomic analysis, stable isotope work, dental calculus analysis and osteological recording. These results can be accessed here alongside a new site report that brings together all the findings and a report that explores the small finds from the site.

Working with Teesside University we have also been specifically analysing one of the wounds on one of the individuals to see if we can determine if it is, in fact, a bite mark inflicted by a large animal.'

It all started in 2004–5 when 82 inhumations and 14 cremated burials were excavated at 3 and 6 Driffield Terrace; all were young male adults on whom cuts to the neck bones of 40 individuals (48.7%) suggested they had been decapitated, although the number of decapitations could have

An exhibition held in York displaying some of the findings. Photo courtesy and © York Archaeological Trust

been higher. The heads belonging to a number of individuals had been placed in the graves in unusual positions, such as near the feet.

Twenty-five of the decapitations exhibited a single cut to the neck. Multiple cut marks on some of the skeletons suggested that the victim was relatively still at the time of assault and the majority of blows were delivered from behind, soon after death. As well as the decapitations, there were three cases of unhealed blade injuries, two to the backs of the hands and one to the femur. Three individuals had cuts to the neck. There was also evidence of large carnivore bite marks on one individual, from a bear, lion or tiger? K. Hunter Mann adds in his *Driffield Terrace An Insight Report* (2015) that the decapitations were 'remarkable' because

> In the rest of Roman Britain, the prevalence of decapitations is about 5% (mostly in rural contexts), usually from the front and probably some time after death. In many cases the

Archaeologists – Kurt Hunter-Mann and colleague – excavating skeletons at Driffield Terrace. Photo courtesy and © York Archaeological Trust

> decapitations were achieved with a single blow, but more than one cut was involved in a number of cases, 11 in one instance. However, the complete removal of the head was not always the primary aim, as in some instances the cut was not complete and the head apparently remained attached to the body.

Kurt Hunter-Mann reveals that most of the deceased seem to have had a violent life, judging from the number of healed injuries:

> Nearly a third of the adults had one or more fractured teeth, mostly upper front teeth and molars (back teeth). The majority of the upper tooth fractures were on the left side, indicating a blow from a right-handed opponent wielding a blunt object. The back tooth fractures were more evenly

distributed and can be attributed to blows delivered to the chin or to teeth clenching. Thirteen individuals had healed cranial trauma, and there were a couple of cases of possible peri-mortem blunt force injuries to the cranium. Trauma to the rest of the body included a fractured scapula blade; several fractures of vertebral processes; a healed blade cut to the left thigh; two fibula fractures; and five metacarpal fractures, all in the right hand. There was also a high prevalence of broken ribs. Fractured clavicles, wrists, ulnas and a vertebra suggest injuries due to falls, whereas fractures and soft tissue injuries evident in the feet and ankles indicate twisted ankles. Stress injuries indicative of an active lifestyle were also common.

YAT continues:

> Finds include an 'unusual pair of iron rings around the ankles of one young male which cannot be regarded as fetters in any normal sense [they were not linked and so probably did not act as leg irons]. There was also a small group of material including a set of miniature silver smiths' tongs which may have been offerings' … [The iron rings

The decapitated skeleton with shackles round his ankles

Detail of the iron rings

A typical decapitation with the head beside the torso. All Courtesy and © York Archaeological Trust

were on] a young male aged between 26 and 35 years (skeleton 3DT37/4344, grave 4352). His decapitated body formed part of a double burial. His bones told the story of an injury-prone life, as well as one that might have been painful due to an abnormality of growth in his right scapula. His injuries included skull fractures, soft tissue damage to his right hand, and a broken left leg. At the time of his death he had an active chest infection.

Gladiators in the arena; a *retiarius* stabs at a *secutor* with his trident in this mosaic from the villa at Nennig, Germany, *c.* second–third century AD

Were the skeletons those of gladiators, soldiers, criminals or slaves? YAT concludes

> The high proportion of younger adult males and frequency of violent trauma could indicate they were gladiators. The demographic profile at Driffield Terrace most closely resembles a burial ground of the second and third century AD at Ephesus, in ancient Greece. Excavated in 1993, this has been interpreted as a burial ground for gladiators.

They were probably not slaves as the skeletons were found in a cemetery for the relatively well off. Soldiers they could well have been as the deceased all complied with the minimum height in force for recruitment.

Equally fascinating is how YAT tells us that

> The face of a man of Central European origin excavated at Driffield Terrace has been digitally reconstructed in partnership with the Centre for Anatomy and Human Identification of the University of Dundee. Facial reconstructions are made by specialist forensic anthropologists who rely on measurements and landmarks (standard reference points) on the human skull to add the missing layers of muscle to the bone. This allows them to reconstruct the contours of a person's face, including the shape of the eyes, nose and mouth. A forensic artist then adds details such as eye and skin colour and possible hairstyles.

> Few of the burials included grave goods. Some had complete pottery vessels, pairs of hobnailed shoes; a bone hairpin, a miniature silver tong and some glass sherds, a bridle cheek-piece, a copperalloy pelta mount, an iron pen nib or goad and a fragment of a pipe clay figurine. The odd single animal bone indicated a joint of meat, to keep the occupant going on his journey to the afterlife; the masses of horse bone deposited in two graves were also grave goods.

York Press (19 January 2016) adds to the intrigue

> Despite variation in isotope levels which suggested some of the 80 lived their early lives outside Britain, most had genomes similar to an Iron Age woman from Melton, East Yorkshire ... the analysis reveals that one of decapitated Romans grew up in the region of modern day Palestine, Jordan or Syria before migrating here and meeting his death in York.

https://www.yorkpress.co.uk/news/14214758.so-who-were-yorks-decapitated-gladiators-researchers-have-new-answers-and-striking-photos/

Unusual grave goods elsewhere include an ivory-handled fan at the railway station cemetery and a club-wielding Hercules from a burial near Peasholme Green.

Child murder?

To modern sensitivities, the discovery of dead infants, however ancient, is naturally abhorrent. However, the Romans seems to have become relatively inured to infant mortality, probably because infant mortality was so prevalent. The skeleton of a baby found in the remains of a barrack block beneath Blake Street was unusual because of its discovery in a military setting. Babies were often buried in houses because they were not considered complete humans and so did not need a formal burial in a cemetery. To find one in a barracks is unusual and may suggest that it was votive offering.

Then there is the report of the skeleton unearthed from a shallow pit at the Vindolanda Roman fort, in 2010. Dr Trudi Buck, a biological anthropologist at Durham University, was unable to determine whether it was a boy or girl but it is believed that the child, aged about 10 and who was tied up, died from a blow to the head and that the body was surreptitiously concealed. The pit has been dated to the mid-third century, when the IVth Cohort of Gauls were in the garrison.

Tests on the child's tooth enamel showed that the child grew up in the Mediterranean. 'Until the child was at least seven or eight, he or she must have been in southern Europe or even North Africa,' Dr Buck said. Patricia Birley, director of the Vindolanda Trust, added: 'This definitely looks like a case of foul play. It has been very sad to find a child in this shallow grave under the barrack floor.'

The exposure or abandonment of infants, particularly female and malformed infants, was commonplace. It was not until AD 374 that child exposure was outlawed when infanticide became the legal equivalent of murder. In an earlier bid to restrict the practice, Constantine had offered free food and clothing to new parents and legalized the sale of babies, mainly into slavery, in AD 329. However, it was still going on some years later: the skeletons of 100 or so infants were excavated from the bottom of a drain in Ashkelon dating from the sixth century AD.

Pott's Disease – tuberculous spondylitis – extrapulmonary TB affecting the spine – has been found in skeletons in York.

Trade and industry

Eboracum would have supported a wide range of industries. Production included military pottery until the mid-third century – military tile kilns have been found in the Aldwark and Peasholme Green areas, ceramic vessels for melting glass indicating glassworking at 16–22 Coppergate, metalworks and leatherworks producing military equipment in Tanner Row. Interestingly, the industries in Coppergate and Tanner Row survived into the early twentieth century. Eboracum was also the place to go for Whitby jet or *gagates* in Latin. From the early third century it was used in jewellery and exported from here throughout Britain and into the wider empire. Examples excavated show jet to have been fashioned into rings, bracelets, necklaces, and pendants depicting, for example, married couples and Medusa. There are fewer than twenty-five jet pendants found so far in the entire Roman world, but six of these come from Eboracum and are held in the Yorkshire Museum. On the approach road to the fortress remains of the legionary pottery and tile kilns have been unearthed.

York is fortunate to be rich in jet from the Roman period; indeed, to the Romans it possessed magical qualities. Pliny the Elder (AD 23–79 *Natural History* 36, 34) gives us the geological, medical and magical properties of the mineral the Romans called *gagates*:

> Gagates is a stone, so called from Gages, the name of a town and river in Lycia. It is said, too, that at Leucolla the sea throws it up, and that it is found over a space twelve stadia inland. It is black, smooth, light, and porous, looks like wood, is of a brittle texture, and gives off a bad smell when

A third- or fourth-century oval jet pendant showing showing Medusa (upper right); a Roman couple (upper left); family group with young boy (lower). Originally published in Lindsay Allason Jones, *Roman Jet in the Yorkshire Museum*, York 1996. Images courtesy and © York Museums Trust

rubbed. You cannot rub off marks made on pottery with this stone. When burnt, it smells of sulphur; and it is a fact that it ignites when in contact with water, while oil quenches it. Its burning fumes repel snakes and dispel hysteria; it can detect symptoms of epilepsy, and is a test of virginity. A decoction of this stone in wine cures tooth-ache; and, in combination with wax, it is good for scrofula. The magicians,

The processes involved in fashioning jet above the door of the old workshop in the Whitby Jet Heritage Centre. Nothing much would have changed since Roman times

it is said, make use of gagates in the practice of what they call axinomancy [divination by axes] assuring us us that it will be sure not to burn if the thing the party desires is about to happen.

https://www.whitbyjet.co.uk/about-jet-read-more; 123B Church Street Whitby

Much evidence for the working and manufacture of jet from the second to the fourth century has been unearthed, although the boom in fashionability came with the third century. One of the star finds is the little bear pendant excavated a Bootham in 1845 along with a coin of

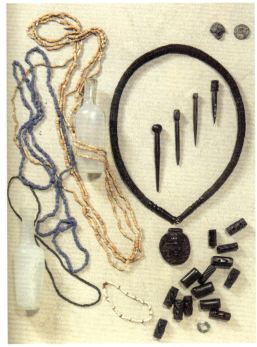

These images show just some of the many jet exhibits in the Yorkshire Museum, and matching beads and hairpins, armlet and bone objects. Originally published in Lindsay Allason-Jones, *Roman Jet in the Yorkshire Museum*, York 1996; courtesy and © Yorkshire Museum

Constantine dated 312–5. The popularity is probably due to the proximity of deposits and the arrival of Julia Domna, empress to Severus, in the city. York's jet jewellery had an empire-wide market if the many articles exported to and found in Cologne are anything to go by.

Other cottage industries included weaving and flax spinning, as evidenced by the spindle dug up at Bishophill Senior.

Julia Domna, fashionable wife of Severus

The Romans are in the Undercroft

In 1966 a survey of the fabric of York Minster identified signs of weaknesses that required immediate remedial work to prevent the collapse of the central tower. It had long been known that the present Minster and its predecessors had been built on the site of the *principia* (headquarters building) of Eboracum's legionary fortress. The underpinning of the tower was subject to continuous archaeological supervision to ensure that historical evidence could be recorded in detail and, where practical, preserved.

A conjectural plan of the *principia* as depicted in the Undercroft Museum

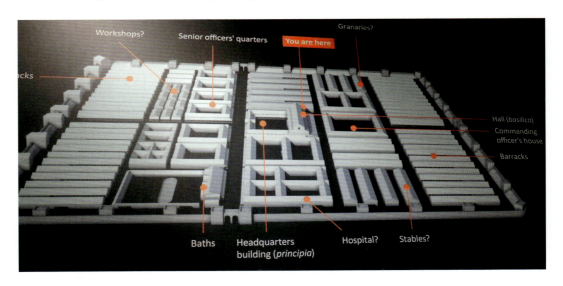

Much of this evidence is now on view in the Minster Undercroft Museum. Access to the Museum is through the Minster's main public entrance, currently in the West Front. The Museum covers all periods of the site's history with the Roman period superbly represented.

The siting and history of the *principia* takes the shape of a series of static and interactive displays, including background information on the role of Eboracum in Roman Britain and the wider Empire. A number of *in situ* remains of Roman buildings – including the *principia,* basilica and what is probably the Commandant's House can be seen.

Heaps of animal bones – pig and sheep – have been unearthed and radiocarbon-dated to the late fourth or early fifth century; this and some

Parts of the superb wall painting. It was found in what would have been the officers' mess

Roof tile made by tilers attached to Legio VI; excavated 1997; the short stabbing sword was made of iron and excavated 1967–72

Stone balls which when hurled became deadly projectiles. The eagle was the symbol of the legion, probably the IXth in this case

Parts of the superb wall painting, continued. It is in three parts: the lower part is designed to resemble marble; the middle is decorated with various figures and scenery while the top is a decorative frieze

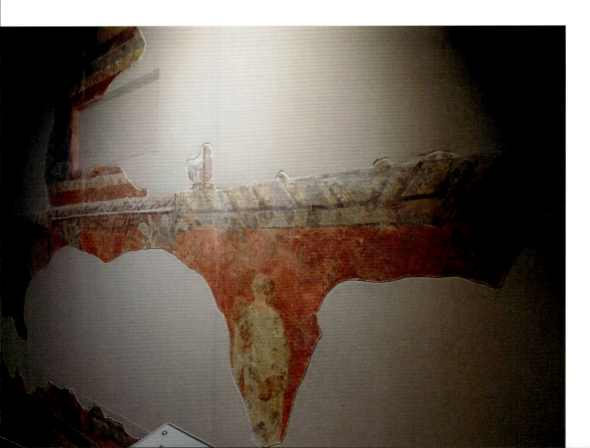

evidence of metal working in hearths suggest a major change in use of the basilica in the final days of the garrison as it prepared to withdraw from York and returned to Rome. Excavation at the Minster in the 1960s and '70s suggests that the basilica may have endured until demolition well before the late eighth or early ninth century as previously believed.

One of the most significant findings was the toppled seven-metre long Roman column now opposite the South Door of the Minster. Substantial remains of painted wall plaster still attached to the wall it was part of were also discovered. This reconstructed wall features a scene with painted figures in vivid colours.

The Headquarters building

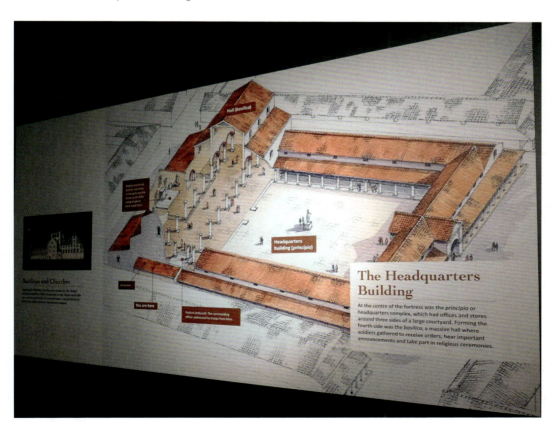

THE ROMANS ARE IN THE UNDERCROFT   119

The Yorkshire Museum

This celebrated museum is one of the best in the UK for Roman and mediaeval exhibits. The museum was founded by the Yorkshire Philosophical Society to house its geological and archaeological collections; it soon outgrew its original premises in Ousegate and in 1828 the society received by royal grant 10 acres of land belonging to St Mary's Abbey on which to build a new museum. It was officially opened in February 1830, which makes it one of the longest established museums in England.

The archaeology collection has almost a million objects that date from around 500,000 BC to the twentieth century. Most of the objects from the Roman, Anglo-Scandinavian and Medieval periods are from the York and Yorkshire area. Following a 2010 refurbishment, the first gallery displayed parts of the Roman collection, focusing on objects from Eboracum, and there is a vivid interactive display describing the lives of some of the Romans whose remains have been found in York. The final record of the famous lost Roman legion, the IXth legion, is on display as part of the Roman gallery. The stone inscription, which has been dated to between 10 December AD 107 and 9 December 108, commemorates the legion's rebuilding in stone of the south-eastern wall of Eboracum's legionary fortress. The BBC reports that 'Experts have described it the finest example of Romano British inscription in existence'.

The stunning life-size statue of Mars, god of war, confronts you as you enter the museum. He is wearing full armour and is carrying a shield. He has a sword on his hip and in his other hand he probably was carrying a metal spear. The statue would have been painted in bright colours. Mars

Mars – god of war. Photo courtesy of and © York Museums Trust

was dug up in 1880 along with three altars in the grounds of the Bar Convent next to Micklegate Bar. Did they come from a nearby temple to Mars, hastily buried to safeguard them from barbarians or Christians?

Along with Mars the large number of Roman finds now housed in the Yorkshire Museum include:

The Legio IX inscription: a superb fortress inscription from one of the main gates of the Roman fortress and one of the best examples of epigraphy to emerge from Roman Britain (*RIB* 665).

It was found seven metres down in King's Square, at the corner of the square and Goodramgate – within a few metres of the site of the Roman south-east gateway.

The inscription reads:

> The Emperor Caesar Nerva Trajan Augustus, son of the deified Nerva, Conqueror of Germany, Conqueror of Dacia, pontifex maximus, in his twelfth year of tribunician power,

Image courtesy of and © York Museums Trust

six times acclaimed emperor, five times consul, father of his country, built this gate by the the IXth Legion Hispana.

We have already mentioned the temple set up by Hieronymianus for Serapis and the altar dedicated by the river pilot M. Minucius Audens. The museum also has the following epigraphical treasures:

An altar erected by the wife of **Quintus Antonius Isauricus**, Sosia Iuncina, dedicated to Fortuna in the bath house in the *colonia*. Isauricus was Imperial Legate, the most senior officer in Eboracum at the time.

Isauricus altar. Image courtesy and © York Museums Trust

The coffin, complete with cupids, in which Septimius Lucianus laid his wife to rest, **Julia Victorina** and his infant son, Constantius.

Julia Victorina's occupancy of her coffin, found in Castle Yard, was short-lived as the centurion's wife and her four year old son, Constantius, were evicted to make way for a male gypsum burial (*RIB* 683, 685). The centurion was a former soldier in the praetorian guard, Septimius Lupianus presumably attached to the VIth legion. The invading corpse was deliberately positioned so as to obscure Julia's inscription, as was that of **Aurelius Super**, centurion of the VIth legion (*RIB* 670) found in 1835 in York Castle yard:

To the spirits of the departed (and) to Aurelius Super, centurion of the Sixth Legion, who lived 38 years, 4 months, 13 days; his wife, Aurelia Censorina, set up this memorial.

Standard-bearer **L. Duccius Rufinus** who died age 28; he was born in Vienne in Gaul and came to York with the IXth legion; we see him on a tombstone found in 1686 in Trinity Gardens, behind Holy Trinity Church in Micklegate, standing proudly with his maniple standard in one hand and writing tablets (*codex ansatus*, his will?) in the other (*RIB* 673). Rufinus is a good example of the diverse origins of the Roman military in the empire, and we shall see many more, all exemplifying the cosmopolitan nature of the army as the empire spread. On the other hand, the soldiers who came with Julius Caesar were probably mainly from the Italian peninsula.

Rufinus. Image ourtesy and © York Museums Trust

Here is the inscription:

> L(ucius) Duccius
> L(uci) (filius) Volt(inia)
> (tribu) Rufi-
> nus Vien(na)
> signif(er) leg(ionis) VIIII
> an(norum) XXIIX
> h(ic) s(itus) e(st)

Lucius Duccius Rufinus, son of Lucius, of the Voltinian voting-tribe, from Vienne, standard-bearer of the IXth Legion, aged 28, lies buried here.

The family may have been Christians as that inscription *'anima innocentissima'* can also be seen in catacombs in Rome.

A highly unusual tiled tomb made from eight *tegulae* or flat tiles, each with the stamp of Legio IX Hispana. Image courtesy of and © York Museums Trust

Another desperately sad inscription (*RIB* 690) comes with the epitaph for ten month old **Simplicia Florentia** found in a coffin on the south side of the bridge over the railway in Holgate Road in 1838; the coffin contained a skeleton set in gypsum:

To the spirits of the departed (and) of Simplicia Florentina, a most innocent soul (anime inocentissimae) , who lived ten months; her father, Felicius Simplex, made this: centurion of the Sixth Legion Victrix.

Celerinius Vitalis, an adjutant (*cornicularius*), set up an altar to the god of the woods, Silvanus (*RIB* 659). Perhaps he was desperate to get out of his office and into the forests around York. It was found at the Mount with *RIB* 664 in 1884.

> D[eo sancto]
> Silva[no s(acrum)]
> L(ucius) Celerin[i]us

> Vitalis corni(cularius)
> leg(ionis) VIIII His(panae)
>
> v(otum) s(olvit) l(aetus) l(ibens) m(erito)
> et donum hoc donum
> adpertiniat cautum attiggam

To the holy god Silvanus, **Lucius Celerinius Vitalis**, *cornicularius* of the IXth Legion Hispana, with this offering gladly, willingly, and deservedly fulfilled his vow. Let the gift, this very gift, form part: I must beware of touching.

A *corniculārius* or cornicular was an officer who served as the adjutant to a centurion, so named for wearing a cornicule (*corniculum*), a small, horn-shaped badge.

Flavius Bellator – a decurion who died age 29 was found in his coffin; he, or his skeleton, was wearing his official gold ring, set with a ruby (*RIB* 674). He was discovered on the south-west side of the Scarborough Railway Bridge. The inscription is also notable for its reference to Eboracum:

> D(is) M(anibus)
> Fl[a]vi Bellatoris dec(urionis) col(oniae) Eboracens(is)
> vixit annis XXVIIII mensib[us . . .]
> [. .] III [. .] II [. . .]

Aelia Severa, wife (or daughter?) of Caecilius Rufus, decurion; his freedman and heir, Caecilius Musicus, organised the burial. A decurion (Latin: *decurio*) was a cavalry officer in command of a squadron (*turma*) of cavalrymen.

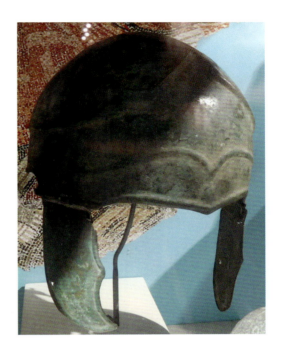

The Chalcidian-style helmet was designed to protect the wearer but also, essentially, to hear commands shouted out or blasts from the *cornu*. Image courtesy of and © York Museums Trust

The museum is also rich in military artefacts including two bronze kettles (essential equipment then as now) stamped with the century that owned it, and a **helmet** dredged from the Tyne.

Perhaps the exhibit with the most impact is **a preserved head of hair**, with jet hairpins and cantharus shaped heads in situ, from a fourth-century inhumation burial found at the railway station booking office site in May 1875. The hair is fashioned into a loose bun. It is exhibits like this which bring Roman York to life, allowing you to experience day to day living and get inside the lives of the Romans.

Image courtesy of and © York Museums Trust

Head pots were all the rage in the early part of the third century. Parts of up to 50 different ones have been excavated in York. They may have been made fashionable during the reign of Septimius Severus and were first produced here by military potters from North Africa around AD 211. This marvellous – and intact – example shows a woman with the hairstyle and facial features modelled on Severus' Syrian wife, Julia Domna, who resided in York with him.

Complete 'Julia Domna style' female head pot. Image courtesy of and © York Museums Trust

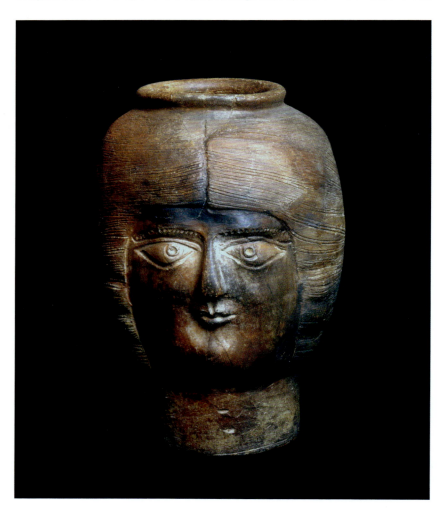

'Millefiori' is Italian for 1000 flowers. It denotes the fine and beautiful decoration formed by joining and stretching coloured strips of glass which are then cut to reveal a pattern. You can see an example of this on a Roman soldier's belt plate – third-century military 'bling'. This was found at 9 Blake Street.

'Julius Alexander's salve for irritations': This domino-sized piece of stone found on the Mount is engraved with the words 'Julius Alexander's salve for irritations', probably infecting the eye. This Roman steatite stamp is known as a collyrium stamp and was used to imprint powdered medicine blocks with their maker's name and function. The words are in reverse, indicating that the stone was used in printing, and is one of only 60 such stamps found world-wide.

Julius Alexander's collyrium stamp

More exhibits in the museum:

A water bucket found on Skeldergate, close to the river Ouse, near a 6-metre-deep wood lined well. Image courtesy of and © York Museums Trust

Ceramic bust of an unknown deity or person found at Fishergate Postern. Courtesy of and © Yorkshire Museum.

Two splendid vases; the one celebrating a good harvest, the other Dionysius – god of wine and orgiastic behaviour. Both were found in Apulia, Italy

The magnificent head of Caracalla (r. AD 198 to 217) who came with his father, Septimius Severus, to Eboracum to learn how to be an emperor

An example of a bronze diploma awarded to a retiring soldier. This granted citizenship and the right to marry to a soldier in the 5th Cohort Raetorum under the command of Sextus Cornelius Dexter from Saldae in Mauretania

Samian ware sherds. All images courtesy of and © York Museums Trust

Samian ware, or *terra sigillata,* is a general term for the ubiquitous fine red Roman pottery roughly translated as 'sealed earth', ie 'clay bearing little images' (*sigilla*), much of it made in Italy and in Gaul, and used and deposited throughout the empire.

This fragment shows two gladiators fighting, in incredible detail. The second image shows another Mars, very different from the one in the doorway.

Images courtesy of and © York Museums Trust

Two examples of *lares* – household gods which were religiously observed in order to bring good fortune and safety to the household; they were integrated into the roofwork of the house.

Both courtesy of and © York Museums Trust

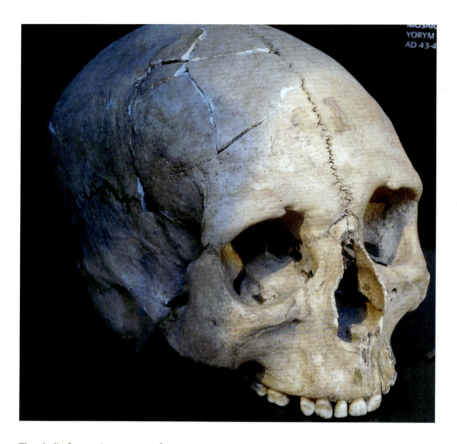

The skull of a carnivorous man from a warm country. Image courtesy of and © York Museums Trust

Osteoarchaeology tells us from his teeth and bones that this man, found in York at Trentholme Drive in 1951, was a meat-eater and lived in a warm climate – perhaps a Berber from Numidia travelling the empire as a mosaic maker from North Africa, the place where some of the finest Roman mosaics survive?

Another star exhibit is the large head of Constantine found in Stonegate.

Constantine. Image courtesy of and © York Museums Trust

The bone plaque inscribed 'Lord Victor, good luck and victory' found on the skeleton of a gladiator or charioteer is, of course, pagan.

The mosaic with a woman's head

If anything characterises Roman culture and interior design it is the wall painting and the quintessentially Roman mosaic.

This impressive section of flooring, probably the floor of a corridor, boasts complex patterns and a woman's face staring straight back at you. According to historyofyork.org.uk/themes/roman/mosaic-with-a-woman-s-head, 'the pupils of her eyes are made from single pieces of rounded black jet and her right cheek-bone and the side of her nose are highlighted in white'. It was found beneath a medieval church floor in Aldwark; her gaze into the future is probably one of the most memorable vestiges of Roman York.

The Ophiotaurus

A fantastic sea creature from a mosaic found in Toft Green. According to its sole classical reference as in Ovid's *Fasti* (3.793 ff), the Ophiotaurus (Ὀφιόταυρος Serpent Bull) was powerful enough to enable whoever slew it and then burnt its entrails to bring down the gods. The monster was killed by an ally of the Titans during the Titanomachy, but the entrails were retrieved by an eagle sent by Zeus before they could be burned. The creature had emerged from Chaos with Gaia and Ouranos.

The Ophiotaurus mosaic

The Four Seasons Mosaic

The magnificent 'Four Seasons Mosaic' was uncovered in 1853 in the course of drainage work at Tanner Row. Three other mosaics were also found in the same house, suggesting someone very wealthy lived there. A coin of the emperor Claudius Gothicus was discovered underneath it, thereby telling us that the mosaic must have been laid down during or after his reign (AD 268–70).

The mosaic depicts the head and shoulders of Medusa who is surrounded by the four seasons. Medusa was a popular image in Roman homes: her petrifying ability to turn people to stone was thought to ward off evil. The four seasons were each shown with items associated with their particular season. Spring is depicted with a bird, Summer with a bunch of grapes, Autumn with a rake and Winter with a bare branch.

The resplendent Four Seasons mosaic

Above: Autumn; below: Winter. Images courtesy and © York Museums Trust

Above: Spring; below: Summer

The grave of a rich lady

In 1901, a stone coffin was discovered near Sycamore Terrace, Bootham. The treasure trove of unusual grave goods found in the coffin is dated to the second half of the fourth century and tell us much about the middle-class Roman obsession with personal appearance and ostentatious display. They include jet, elephant ivory and blue glass bead bracelets, earrings, pendants, and beads. Also in there were a blue glass jug 123 millimetres tall, likely to have contained perfumes, and a glass mirror.

The deceased was a truly wealthy lady as indicated by the exotic (and therefore expensive) provenances of many of the grave goods. Ivory was a rare material in Roman Britain although it has been found in the nearby cemetery discovered during the construction of the railway station in the 1870s. Jet, as we have noted, became very popular in the third and fourth centuries, and may have had associations with the cult of Bacchus and with Christianity. We also can see a fan handle, the frame of a parasol, lamps, keys, spoons and combs as well as pins and brooches and a lot of ceramics. There is a Christian motto in bone: 'Welcome sister, may you live long in god'; this adorned the lady's jewellery box in which she kept her bangles and beads.

'The remains of the "ivory bangle lady" were analysed using standard methods for the assessment of ancestry in forensic anthropology. During the osteological analysis it was noted that the facial characteristics of this female exhibited a mix of "black" and "white" ancestral traits. The skull exhibited a low, wide and broad nasal ridgeand wide inter-orbital breadth suggestive of "black" ancestry, while the nasal spine and nasal border demonstrated "white" characteristics.'

From: Eckardt, Hella et al., 'Lady of York: migration, ethnicity and identity in Roman Britain Antiquity', March 2010.

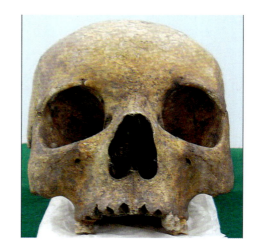

Close-up of the lady's skull

THE YORKSHIRE MUSEUM

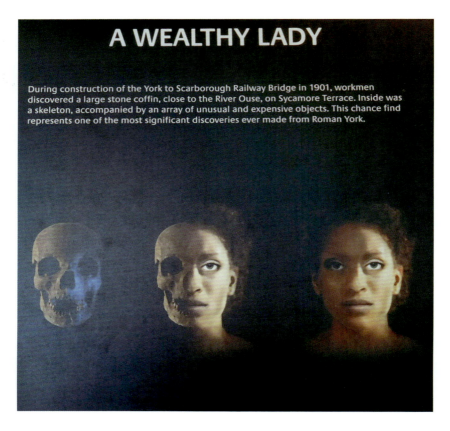

The grave goods. Image courtesy of and © York Museums Trust

The grave with the jewels

Information board describing the exhibit and showing how the deceased's 2000-year-old face was reconstructed

Here are more treasures. They tell us much about Roman religion, life expectancy, the military, the funerary epigraph and demonstrate the wide diversity of York findspots:

Stone altar (*RIB 646*):

The capital and part of the base are lost; found at the north end of the current railway station in 1875. It lay at the head of a skeleton with a glass vessel near by. Described in *Eboracum* as altar, of gritstone, 1ft by 1ft 8ins, by 1ft with the top broken off. Found in 1875, on 'a small pile of stones'.

D] E O GENIO LOCI V(OTVM)] S(OLVIT) L(IBENS) M(ERITO)

to the god, the Genius of the place, willingly and deservedly pays his vow.

Stone statue of a winged deity (*RIB 641*)

Dressed in a fringed skirt this winged figure holds two keys in his left hand, while a serpent acts as a belt and rests its head above his right knee. The right hand and the head are lost. Found under the city wall while building the railway station in 1874. Now in the Yorkshire Museum YORYM: 2007.6162. The dedication reads:

VOL(VSIVS) IRE[NAEVS D(ONVM) [D(EDIT) ARIMANI V(OTVM) [S(OLVENS L(IBENS) M(ERITO)
'Volusius Irenaeus, paying his vow willingly and deservedly to Arimanes, gave (this) gift.'

Eboracum tells us that the dedication is 'to Arimanius, the Mithraic god of Evil. The missing head was most probably that of a lion, symbolic of all-devouring Death. The snake girdle represents the tortuous course of the sun though the sky; the wings signify the winds; while the keys are those of the heavens and the sceptre is the sign of dominion.'

Altar dedicated to Jupiter Optimus Maximus (*RIB 649*)

A limestone altar: on the right side is a weathered figure holding a staff in its left hand. On the left side is a sacrificial scene with a male figure in a knee-length tunic and possibly a hair-band, holding an animal; there is a wreath above this animal. It is now believed that the figure

Arimanius. Image courtesy of and © York Museums Trust

is a military figure in profile facing right wearing a crested helmet and possibly armour, with a band sculpted around his neck. The *RIB* archive tentatively describes the right-side relief as possibly Jupiter ('figure with shaft in left hand, weathered away below waist'), and the left-side relief as Hercules ('figure with ?headdress faces sin. And seems to wrestle with an animal (?lion), corona above. ?Hercules'). Only the first two lines are preserved; it was found in 1638 while digging the foundation of a house on the site at Castlegate where Fairfax House was later built in 1762. Now among the Chandler Marbles, Ashmolean Museum, Oxford. The dedication reads:

> I(ovi) O(ptimo) M(aximo)
> Dis Deabusque
> Hospitalibus Pe-
> natibusq(ue) ob con-
> servatam salutem
> suam suorumq(ue)
> P(ublius) Ael(ius) Marcian-
> us praef(ectus) coh(ortis)
> ARAM SAC ET AVG DE

To Jupiter Best and Greatest, to the gods and goddesses of hospitality and to the Penates, for having kept safe the welfare of himself and of his household, Publius Aelius Marcianus, prefect of the cohort, had this altar set up …

Altar dedicated to Mars (*RIB* 650)

Stone altar found in the Bar Convent, outside Micklegate Bar, in 1880. Now in the Yorkshire Museum YORYM: 2007.6163.

Described in *Eboracum* as 'Altar, of gritstone, 7ins by 1ft by 7ins, found in 1880 in a dump of Roman stones … with burials below them, at St Mary's Convent, Nunnery Lane, close to the main Roman road, just outside the built up area of the Roman town. The stones had been gathered togther after the Roman period'.

DEO MARTI AGRIVS AVSPEX V(OTUM) S(OLVIT) L(IBENS) M(ERITO) 'To the god Mars, Agrius Auspex pays his vow willingly and deservedly.'

RIB 653 is an altar dedicated to the African, Italian, and Gallic mother goddesses

Found in Micklegate, opposite Holy Trinity Church in 1752; in the Yorkshire Museum: YORYM: 1999.254.

Likewise the stone altar *RIB* 654 found in 1850, in Park Place, Monkgate, on the line of the road leading north-east to Malton. In the Yorkshire Museum: YORYM: 2007.6173.

Dedication to the Divinities of the Emperor and to the goddess Joug[...] (*RIB* 656)

Dedication-slab found in 1839 on the site of the bank, at the junction of Nessgate and Ousegate (with *RIB* 648 and 698). Now in the Yorkshire Museum: YORYM: 2007.6196.

Numinib(us) Aug(ustorum) et Deae Ioug.[. . .]- -

sius aedem pro parte di[midia . . .]

To the Divinities of the Emperor and to the goddess Joug.[... ...] sius ... half of the shrine ...

RIB suggests the name of the goddess is formed from Celtic *iougon*, a yoke.

CIL VI 9143: Inscribed tablet dedicated to Calpurnia

Calpurnia L(uci))(mulieris) l(iberta) Hilara / vix(it) an(nos) XXXII / v(ivit) A(ulus) Petronius A(uli) l(ibertus) Alexander / anatiarius sibi et coniugi / suae fecit cum qua concorditer vixit.

RIB 662 is a bronze plate which was originally silvered. *RIB* 663 is stuck to the back found at the site of the old railway station; date about 1840. Greek inscription:

> Θεοῖς
> τοῖς τοῦ ἡγε-
> μονικοῦ πραι-
> τωρίου Σκριβ(ώνιος)
> Δημήτριος

Which translates as:

> To the gods of the legate's residence (*praetorium*) Scribonius Demetrius (set this up).

Demetrius is presumably Demetrius of Tarsus, the *Grammaticus* (scholar), who took part in Plutarch's dialogue *de defectu oraculorum* just before the Pythian festival in AD 83–4 (Plutarch 410A). Demetrius had recently returned from his visit to Britain where he had accompanied a voyage to the Western Islands of Scotland on imperial orders.

RIB 663

> Ὠκεανῶι
> καὶ Τηθύι
> Δημήτρι[ος]

Translation

> To Ocean and Tethys Demetrius (set this up). See above p. 47 for details.

Image courtesy of and © York Museums Trust

Other finds include:

The top part of an altar stone found at the site of the Co-operative Offices, Rougier Street in 1909 (*RIB 657*).

An altar dedicated to Veteris found in the garden of the Bar Convent, outside Micklegate Bar in 1880 (*RIB 660*). Veteris was a Celtic god; during the third century AD the cult was particularly popular among the ranks of the Roman army.

Then there is the dedication (*RIB 666*) slab to Trajan found in 1879 at the north end of the Fine Art Exhibition Building, now the City Art Gallery, north-west of Bootham Bar, the site of one of the Roman gates.

And the one dedicated to Marcus Aurelius (*RIB 667*) excavated during digging the foundations for the Mechanics' Institute in Clifford Street.

Nine building stones of the VIth legion (*RIB 669*) were built into the lower courses of the inner face of the Multangular Tower. They read:

a leg(io) [VI] Vic[t(rix)] *b* leg(io) [VI] Vict(rix) *c* Calp]urni Vict[o]rini *d* Anton(i) Prim(i)

N CXX *e* Anton(i) Prim(i) *f* VNO [. . .] MNVI [. . . .] VIC *g* [. . .] *h* LN [.] XXX *i* [. . .]

a-e translate as

a [VIth] Legion Victrix *b* [VIth] Legion Victrix *c* The century of Calpurnius Victorinus. *d* The century of Antonius Primus (built) 120 (feet). *e* The century of Antonius Primus.

A stone coffin was discovered at the Castle yard in 1835 bearing the inscription (*RIB* 670):

Aur(elio) Supero cent(urioni)
leg(ionis) VI qui vixit an(n)is
XXXVIII m(ensibus) IIII d(iebus) XIII Aurelia Censorina co(n)iunx
memoriam possuit

which means

To the spirits of the departed (and) to Aurelius Super, centurion of the VIth Legion, who lived 38 years, 4 months, 13 days; his wife, Aurelia Censorina, set up this memorial.

In 1872 a tombstone was excavated from under the road opposite the current railway station, reading 'To the memory of … Bassaeus Julius and of his very sweet son Felix'. (*BIR* 672). The tombstone of Titus Flavius Flavinus, centurion of the Sixth Legion Victrix, was erected by his heir, Classicius Aprilis; Flavinus ordered this before his death (*RIB* 675) It was found at the end of Rawcliffe Lane in 1927. *RIB* 677 shows that Valerius Theodorianus, of Nomentum, who lived 35 years, 6 months had his tomb set up by Emilia Theodora, his mother and heir. His coffin was found in the early 1800s in R. Driffield's garden at the Mount.

> G(aio) ...]o G(ai) fil(io)
> [Cl(audia)] (tribu) [... N]ovaria
> [... leg(ionis) I]X Hisp(anae) here-
> [des et lib(erti)] patrono
> [bene mer]enti fecerunt

To Gaius ..., son of Gaius, of the Claudian voting-tribe, from Novaria, ... of the IXth Legion Hispana, his heirs and freedmen set this up to their own well-deserving patron.

This is the inscription found at the Mount in 1852 (*RIB* 680). Novaria (modern Novara) lies west of Milan, and belonged to *Claudia tribus*. As the VIth Legion replaced the IXth Hispana at York about AD 120, the deceased must have died by that time, or, if in retirement, within a few years of that date.

RIB 682 is the funerary inscription for Aelia Aeliana, found during the building of the current railway station in 1872. It is of special interest because, as *RIB* says:

> In a shell-niche, carrying on the spandrel some scroll-work flanked by two dolphins, stands a couch on which recline, on the right, a man who in his left hand holds a scroll and has his right hand resting on the shoulder of his wife who in her left hand holds a goblet. A young girl stands at the left-hand end of the high-backed couch. A small costrel [leather bottle] lies on the floor under the couch, and in the foreground stands a three-legged table with claw-feet, laden with food.

RIB 684 is a funerary inscription for 13-year-old Corellia Optata found at the Mount in 1861.

It reads:

> [D(is)] M(anibus)
> Corellia Optata an(norum) XIII
> Secreti Manes qui regna

Acherusia Ditis incoli-
tis quos parva petunt post
lumina vite exiguus cinis et simulacrum corpo(r)is um-
bra insontis gnate geni-
tor spe captus iniqua
supremum hunc nate
miserandus defleo finem
Q(uintus) Core(llius) Fortis pat(er) f(aciendum) c(uravit)

Which translates as

To the spirits of the departed: Corellia Optata, aged 13. You mysterious spirits who dwell in Pluto's Acherusian realms, and whom the meagre ashes and the shade, empty semblance of the body, seek, following the brief light of life; father of an innocent daughter, I, a pitiable victim of

The Corellia inscription. Image courtesy of and © York Museums Trust

unfair hope, bewail her final end. Quintus Corellius Fortis, her father, had this set up.

A large glass vessel inside the coffin, sealed with lead, contained Corellia's ashes. The reference to Dis – god of the underworld – and Acheron – one of the rivers of the underworld – make this epitaph particularly vivid and pathetic, and would have reminded readers of Book VI of Virgil's *Aeneid*, as well as other descriptions of the underworld.

This sad epitaph for mother and daughter (*RIB* 686) set up by husband and father was found in 1892 on the site of the Mount Hotel, beside the Roman road leading south-west to Tadcaster. The draped figure of **Julia Brica** stands in the niche holding what looks like a cup. At her right side stands the draped figure of her daughter, holding in her right hand an object, perhaps a pet.

It reads:

The epitaph for Julia Brica and her daughter

>D(is) M(anibus)
>Iulie Brice an(norum) XXXI
>Sepronie Martine an(norum) VI
>Sepronius Martinus f(aciendum) c(uravit)

To the spirits of the departed (and) of Julia Brica, aged 31, and of Sepronia Martina, aged 6, Sepronius Martinus had this set up.

Julia Fortunata's sarcophagus. Image courtesy of and © York Museums Trust

Julia Fortunata, celebrated in *RIB* 687, was from Sardinia. Her husband, Verecundius Diogenes, set up the tomb, perhaps quoting a hexameter written by Catullus (lxii, 54) in his last line. It was unearthed during the building of the railway station. Verecundius Diogenes was a *sevir augustalis*; these magistrates looked after the cult of the emperor's divinity – a symbol of loyalty – ceremony and entertainment. Diogenes hailed from Bourges, southern France. The sarcophagus was found near Scarborough Bridge – but it contained the skeleton of a man. A good example of the recycling of sarcophagi which, if anything would have been cheaper when second hand – sold as having one careful owner?

> Iul(iae) Fortunate domo
> Sardinia Verec(undio) Dio-
> geni fida coniuncta
> marito

To the memory of Julia Fortunata from Sardinia; (she was) a loyal wife to her husband, Verecundius Diogenes.

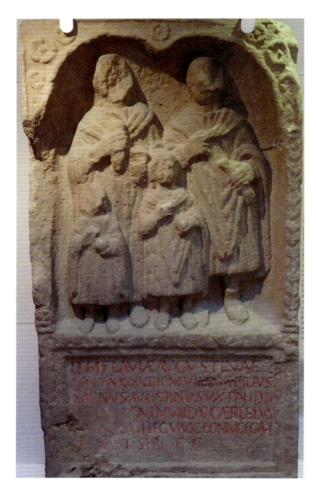

This tomb, found on the Mount, shows a triple tragedy commemorated by ex-soldier Quintus Corellius Fortis for his wife, Flavia Augustina, and his two infant children. Perhaps this is how Corellius liked to think how things might have turned out, had Flavia lived. Image courtesy of and © York Museums Trust

RIB 695 is another child death – this time of three-year-old Crescens buried with his 30-year-old mother, Eglecta. The right-hand side of the tombstone was found built into the south wall of All Saints' Church, North Street about 1682 while the left was discovered while the church was being underpinned in 1931.

The inscription reads: To the spirits of the departed (and) to Eglecta, aged 30, here buried beside their son Crescens, aged 3; Antonius Stephanus had this set up to his wife.

RIB 696: to her child, [who] lived 13 years, the mother, Vitellia Procula, as heir in part, [set this up].

A rare Roman embrace. Many epitaphs and tombs were rather formulaic with compliments and epithets trotted out as if picked coldly from a mason's catalogue. This, though, seems genuine because it gives a rare picture of contact between the man and wife

This had been reused in a medieval building and spotted in 1865 in a heap of rubble near Ebor Street, Clementhorpe, on the west bank of the River Ouse and south-east of the Roman *colonia*.

The Roman Bath Museum

The Roman Bath Museum is child friendly and hands-on. It is in St Sampson's Square, beneath the Roman Bath public house. The main feature of the museum is the remains of part of a legionary bath house in the southern quadrant of the fortress.

This bath house was excavated in 1930–1; it is probably of the early fourth century AD and was originally only viewable through a glass panel in the floor of the public house. Now visible to visitors to the museum

Roman Bath Museum – The amazingly well preserved hypocaust in the museum in 2022

are the east corner and south-east side of a *frigidarium* including a cold plunge bath together with part of the *caldarium* (heated room), with an apse and hypocaust system (underfloor heating). The cold plunge bath has a tiled floor with some of the tiles bearing stamps of the two legions that occupied the fortress, the IXth and the VIth. It is probable that the large Roman sewer discovered under Swinegate served this bath house. Set among the excavated remains are descriptive displays, original Roman artefacts and a collection of replica uniforms, clothing, regalia and equipment. The splendidly detailed replica helmets are of particular interest. Visitors are encouraged to try on the outfits and to handle the reproduction military equipment. The museum has a small souvenir and book shop.

York's huge public bath house occupied the southern corner of the fortress with its 9,100 square metres at the north-east end of Micklegate.

Gambling was rife in the baths, as evidenced by the discovery of bone and pottery counters in the sewer silt. A water pipe found at Wellington Row and a fountain at Bishophill attest to a piped water supply to bath houses and the grander residences. Water for most of the town was from wells, a fine example having been excavated in Skeldergate.

DIG YORK

DIG is a hands-on archaeological adventure run by York Archaeological Trust giving children and young adults the chance to become trainee 'diggers' and discover the most exciting artefacts from 2000 years of York's history. Tours last one hour. DIG is in the now redundant St Saviour's church and offers four special in-door excavation pits, all based on real-life digs in the city and filled with replica Roman, Viking, medieval and Victorian finds. The website (https://digyork.com/what-is-dig/) says

> Kids can dig down deep in the synthetic, no messy soil to discover artefacts from the four major periods of York's fascinating history. An archaeologist is on hand to answer your questions on your finds and help you piece together what it would have been like to live in the [Roman] past. Kids can get hands on with history and actually touch finds from previous YAT digs, including pottery, bone and even antlers! You will discover what these artefacts tell us about the lives of people who used them.

A good example of YAT-DIG activities was the 2018 Tang Hall Exhibition which demonstrated how the discovery of Roman artefacts in the city, including the remains of a kiln found just outside modern York and pottery discoveries at a burial site on Tadcaster Road, can tell us so much about the lives of the Romans. Local residents of Tang Hall took part in Roman pottery creating sessions led by famous potter and experimental archaeologist Graham Taylor from 'Potted History'.

Some of the splendid pots produced in Tang Hall
Young archaeologists at DIG

Eboracum Annual Roman Festival

Every year over one weekend in late spring York holds its annual Eboracum Roman Festival. The principal events take place in the grounds of York Museum Gardens which surround the Yorkshire Museum. Eboracum comes to life, literally. Visitors find themselves face to face with legionary soldiers and their families in a colourful and bustling tented encampment. Younger visitors (and the young at heart) can become Romans for a while, trying on armour and costumes and taking part in various Roman-themed craft activities. All ages can enjoy Roman cookery, weaponry and craft demonstrations given by the many re-enactment groups present.

Daily parades of soldiers and their followers march their way through the historic streets of York, walking in the footsteps of the original Romans and early Britons two thousand years ago. Military drill demonstrations take place in front of the Yorkshire Museum together with displays of Roman fashion, dancing and falconry. Knowledgable and expert Roman-costumed guides take visitors on walking tours which show many of the Roman sights in the city.

Pictures courtesy of Legio VI Victrix. Members of the Roman re-enactment group 'Legio VI Victrix' in York's Museum Gardens taking part in the Eboracum Roman Festival

EBORACUM ANNUAL ROMAN FESTIVAL 165

A life in the day of a Roman in York II: A letter from the edge of empire

Javolenus Priscus had a younger brother who was in the Roman army; Octavius Priscus was a Legion Legate in the IXth Hispana Legion based in Eboracum under Agricola, Imperial Legate and Governor of Britannia.

The IXth legion was about 5,500 men strong; the usual six military tribunes reported to Octavius as well as the commander of the camp and various staff officers in charge of engineers, stores, weapons, priests, musicians, medical support and record keepers. The cavalry commanders also reported to him.

Twenty years or so earlier the legion had suffered serious casualties at the battle of Camulodunum (modern Colchester), when Boudica, queen of the Iceni tribe, revolted against Roman rule.

By AD 80 Octavius Priscus and the IXth were in the front line, ready for Agricola's invasion of Caledonia. They had taken the Scottish lowlands and controlled the land between the Tyne-Solway and the Forth-Clyde isthmuses inhabited by the Votadini and Selgovae, pushing as far north as the Tavus, the river Tay. They had another lucky escape when, according to Tacitus, the Caledonians surprised the Romans in a night attack on their fort. The Caledonians burst in striking panic amongst the Romans, slaying the sentries. But Agricola sent his cavalry in to save the legion. The legion responded, took heart and fought for their honour, repelling the Caledonians.

Inspired by this success, the Romans pushed north for the decisive battle of Mons Graupius, near the Moray Firth. Flushed by the success of the IXth Hispana, Octavius Priscus describes the battle and its preamble in a letter to his brother, Javolenus now back in Rome after his time in Eboracum:

Salve.

I pray to the Lares, the household gods of my present billet that I may find you and our whole family in good health.

The news is that we have just defeated the Britons at the battle here at Mons Graupius, a godless and desolate place many miles from anything you could call civilisation. Our victory surely means that Britannia is now ours and we can get on with the business of Romanisation. Perhaps our next target will be Hibernia, a large island off the west coast.

You might like to know that in the centre our auxiliary infantry numbered 8,000 men flanked by 3,000 cavalry; the Roman legionaries were in front of their camp in reserve. Altogether our army was 23,000 men strong. The Caledonian army was led by a chieftain called Calgacus, 30,000 strong, some of whom were on higher ground rising up in tiers in a kind of horseshoe formation. Their chariots sped about in no man's land. Spears from both sides filled the air before Agricola ordered the auxiliaries to launch a frontal attack: four cohorts of Batavians and two cohorts of Tungrian swordsmen clashed with the Caledonians, stabbing them in their faces; they were soon all cut down on the lower slopes of the hill. The enemy chariots were dealt with by our cavalry. An outflanking movement by the barbarians further up the hill failed when they themselves were outflanked by four squadrons of cavalry which Agricola had wisely held in reserve for just such an eventuality. The routed Caledonians fled into a nearby wood and were pursued mercilessly and relentlessly by Roman units. 10,000 Caledonians fell that day; we lost a mere 360 auxiliary troops. Our legions in reserve had no cause to intervene.

Will write again soon, perhaps from Hibernia.

adapted from *How to be a Roman – A life in the day of a Roman* family by Paul Chrystal, 2017

The 1900th anniversary of the founding of Eboracum in 1971

The Queen and the Duke of Edinburgh visited York on 28 June 1971 to celebrate the 1,900th anniversary of the founding of York by Roman governor Petillius Cerialis and named Eboracum by geographer Ptolemy. The year of celebration included a re-enactment of the cremation of Emperor Severus after a torchlight procession(!)

Commemorative postage stamp for the 1900th anniversary

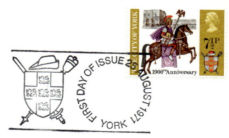

Hoards found in York

A number of hoards have been found in and around York; they include

The Wold Newton Hoard – 'a once in a lifetime find'

One day in 2014 metal detectorist David Blakey was out detecting near the village of Wold Newton, East Yorkshire when he came across this hugely important hoard.

The quick-witted David Blakey filmed its discovery and immediately reported it to the Portable Antiquities Scheme (PAS) rather than just emptying it out. This has allowed archaeologists the rare opportunity to excavate it in different layers to see how different coins were added to the vessel.

As the museum website tells us:

> insect remains attached to some of the coins also offer another way of analysing the contents. All this means there is huge potential for getting a greater understanding of the period and why it was buried. [To] find out more about the discovery and recording of the hoard [go to] the blog entry by PAS Finds Liaison Officer Rebecca Griffiths.

The website continues:

> The hoard can be dated quite precisely, with the latest coins in the hoard suggesting it was hidden in 307. This is shortly after the death of the emperor Constantius in York, and the rise to power of his son, Constantine the Great. The hoard provides a link to events which would reshape the empire and the history of Europe.
>
> The Wold Newton hoard is the largest of that period found in northern Britain. It contains 1,857 copper coins which were concealed within a ceramic pot. This is a large store of wealth, roughly equivalent to a legionary's annual salary, three year's salary for a carpenter or six years for a farm labourer. It could buy 700 chickens, 2,000 of the finest fish or 11,000 pints of beer!

The Wold Newton Hoard on permanent display in the museum. Image courtesy of and © York Museums Trust

The Blake Street Hoard

The Blake Street hoard of 35 silver denarii was found during archaeological digs within the fortress of York in the 1970s. Its numismatic dating suggests a deposit from the earliest Roman activity in York, with the latest coin dating to AD 74, although stratigraphic dating now throws this into doubt.

The Haxby Hoard

In 2014, 350 or so bronze nummi were found in a single pot just outside Haxby, north of York. These coins emanate from mints across the empire: France, Germany, Italy and the near East; there are over 60 different mint marks present which dates it from AD 330–47. Three different emperors are represented: Constantine I, Constantine II, and Constans, as well as the personification of the cities Constantinopolis and Rome. The hoard demonstrates that wealth in Roman Britain was not confined to the towns and cities; this was probably the savings of one individual and is now in the Yorkshire Museum.

In 1998 a hoard of twenty Roman bronze coins was dug up, also near Haxby. Aerial photography has shown the probable existence of Roman ditches at Haxby Lodge Farm, Moor Lane. Roman *tegula* (roof tiles) have also been excavated in the area.

A coin from the Haxby Hoard

Grave goods found in Heslington. Originally published in Lindsay Allason-Jones, *Roman Jet in the Yorkshire Museum*, York 1996; courtesy and © Yorkshire Museum

The Overton Hoard

The hoard comprises a collection of 37 silver Roman coins (denarii) and was discovered in September 2016 on land near Overton near York along with fragments of pottery. The coins range from Domitian (AD 81–96) to the reign of Septimius Severus (AD 193–211).

The Heslington Hoard

The huge Heslington Hoard is a mid-fourth-century AD hoard of 2,795 copper alloy nummi. It was found in 1966 during the construction of the University of York's Alcuin College. Over half of the hoard is made up of contemporary copies of official Roman coinage, and there are 279 overstruck coins.

Heslington has also yielded up grave goods comprising mixed jewellery in a grave in Heslington Field.

The Ryedale Hoard

The Yorkshire Museum celebrated its reopening in April 2022 with an exhibition featuring the splendid Ryedale Hoard, a discovery which displays what are now some of Yorkshire's most significant Roman objects. The objects include an 1,800-year old bust of the Roman Emperor Marcus Aurelius. 'For the very first time in Yorkshire, visitors will be able see this exciting new discovery and explore the mystery of who buried the Hoard and why.'

The museum website goes on to explain that the 13cm bust is part of a collection of bronze objects found by metal detectorists James Spark and Mark Didlick in a field near Ampleforth in Ryedale, North Yorkshire, in May 2020.

Items of the Ryedale Hoard, courtesy York Museums Trust

We have American donor Richard Beleson to thank for the purchase of the Ryedale Roman Hoard, with additional funding through Art Fund and a number of individual donors. This enabled York Museums Trust to make the purchase from David Aaron, who originally acquired the hoard at auction.

What's in the hoard? The three bronzes and a plumb bob date from the later second century AD; these offer a rare insight into religious ceremony in rural Roman Yorkshire; the burial of these objects would have been a votive offering to the gods.

The bust of Marcus Aurelius (r. AD 161–180) would have been fixed on the top of a sceptre or priestly staff and carried by the leader of local religious ceremonies. As such it is 'a potent symbol of the Imperial Cult, the empire-wide worship of emperors as divine. Such direct evidence of the imperial cult is exceedingly rare, especially in rural settings like this. The bust is absolutely unique, exceedingly rare and of great national significance in its own right'.

The three objects found alongside the bust add context to the burial: The horse and rider figure is beautifully detailed; a localised depiction of the god Mars, is of a type that has never been found this far north. The Museum speculates that he knife handle in the form of a horse, 'may symbolically represent a sacrificial animal in this context'. The plumb bob is a fine example of a tool used in Roman construction projects. Its inclusion in the hoard is unique in Roman Britain and may celebrate and give thanks for some local landscape engineering project.

Amazingly, all the artefacts are preserved in outstanding condition, with no corrosion and all for the most part largely complete.

The Museum concludes, 'before the discovery of this hoard, the presence of the Romans in this area was little known. This find therefore rewrites the history of our region. The situation of this discovery, with detailed and reliable provenance information, makes the hoard even more significant'.

Other finds

A gold amulet was found on the site of the old railway station around 1840; it bore two lines, the first with magical characters which remains untranslateable; while the second is ΦΝΕΒΕΝΝΟΥΘ, meaning 'the lord of the gods'.

Amulets *(periamma, periapton, amuletum* or *remedium)* were an important and a pervasive means of delivering magic, mainly on the health care front. People wore them as a (distinctly un-clinical) way of deflecting or curing illness and to ward off the evil eye and other unwelcome intruders on their general well-being.

Masks and costume were an integral part of Roman ritual and cult worship – the masks concealed the identities of the priests involved or assumed the identities of the spirits involved. This fine mask was found at Catterick.

The Catterick masquerade. Image courtesy of and © York Museums Trust

Roman York in the Future

Obviously, one hopes that the sterling work carried out over the last few decades by the York Archaeological Trust, York Museums Trust, York Archaeology and York Civic Trust continues apace and that the conservation, preservation and investigation they all do proceeds well into the future. At the time of writing there are two fascinating projects in the pipeline: one confirmed, the other in the planning stage. Both will do much to establish York as one of the UK's centres of excellence for the enjoyment and study of the Roman period in Britannia.

Road radar to reveal York's Roman secrets: archaeology without a spade or trowel in sight.

Martin Millett, Laurence Professor of Classical Archaeology at Cambridge and a trustee of York Archaeological Trust, describes this groundbreaking project as

> The biggest investigation ever undertaken into Eboracum, the Roman city buried beneath York, is set to begin this summer [2022]. Ground penetrating radar will be used to map as much of the influential ancient settlement as possible in a bid to learn more about its evolving layout and use.
>
> Did the Romans redesign their fortress in the 4th and 5th centuries? What was the settlement [vicus] around it like and how did this change over time? Was Eboracum spruced up when emperors came to town? These are just some of the intriguing questions which Martin Millett and his colleagues hope to answer.

The University Research Press Release [https://www.cam.ac.uk/research/news/road-radar-to-reveal-yorks-roman-secrets] reveals how:

> Over summer 2022, a vehicle equipped with specialist radar equipment will survey 20km of streets around York – the first time a project on this scale has been undertaken in the UK. The team behind the scheme are working with City of York Council to access as much of the city centre road network as possible, including some pedestrianised streets, during the survey, with minimal disruption to the public.
>
> Alongside the road surveys, a different radar system will scan the green spaces in the city centre, particularly around the Yorkshire Museum and York Minster.
>
> The initiative is a joint project between Universities of Cambridge and Reading, York Archaeology and the York Museums Trust funded by the Arts & Humanities Research Council (AHRC). The 30-month-long project aims to collate everything archaeologists and historians know about the whole of Roman York into a single database which will then be made freely available to the public.

He adds that his team will be looking for evidence of Eboracum's architecture and infrastructure being enhanced during periods of imperial residence (AD 208–11 and AD 305–6), or following York's elevation to colonial status in the early third century. As well as the research there will be a series of public engagement projects including volunteer-run research projects, an art initiative and a project for schools around the country linking research findings to geography, physics, geology and archaeology.

A mobile scanning rig in archaeological action

Professor Millett recently led the team which successfully mapped a complete Roman city, Falerii Novi, in Italy, using the same technology. This research received global media coverage.

The Roman Quarter

In January 2022 York Archaeological Trust announced that

> Major City Centre development plans re-submitted – including a new world-class Roman attraction
>
> York-based developers, Rougier Street Developers, in partnership with York Archaeological Trust have submitted plans on developing a major area of York city centre that was once the site of a major Roman Road nearly two thousand years ago.
>
> The development will be called The Roman Quarter and includes plans to knock down three buildings and replace them with Grade A offices, an aparthotel, new homes, and a world-class, Roman-themed tourist attraction.
>
> York Archaeological Trust will conduct a two year dig of the site, prior to building work starting and bringing significant public benefit, creating excitement and engagement amongst York residents and visitors alike, as the layers of history are peeled back.

York Archaeology excavating in a York street. Courtesy of York Archaeology

Roman York timeline

55–54 BC Julius Caesar invades Britain

27 BC–14 AD Caesar Augustus emperor

37–41 AD Caligula emperor; Cunobelinus ruling most of south-east England

41–54 Claudius emperor

43–9 Claudius and Aulus Plautius invade Britain. Conquest of southern Britain. Brigantes become a client-kingdom allied to Rome

43 (August) Romans capture the capital of the Catuvellauni tribe, Colchester

44 (June) Romans take the hills forts of Dorset, including Maiden Castle

47 Romans force their allies, the Iceni tribe of East Anglia, to surrender their weapons. The Iceni resist but their revolt is short lived

48 Romans have now conquered all territory between the Humber estuary and the Severn estuary. Parts that remain under British control include Dumnonii (Cornwell and Devon), Wales and the North West of England.

49 Romans found a *colonia* at Colchester for retired soldiers – the first civilian centre of Roman Britain and – for a time – the capital.

51 The leader of the exiled Catuvellauni tribe, Caratacus, is captured. He has led a long guerrilla war against the Roman forces for years, and was eventually defeated by the Roman governor Publius Ostorius Scapula. Caratacus spent the remainder of his days in in Italy.

54–68 Nero emperor

60 Romans attack the druid stronghold of Anglesey. The campaign to occupy Wales is cut short by the Iceni revolt in south east England.

61 After attempting to fully annexe East Anglia, Boudica leads a rebellion against the Romans. After razing Colchester, London and St Albans, Boudica is eventually defeated at the Battle of Watling Street.

68–9 The Brigantes break with Rome

69–79 Vespasian emperor

71–2 IX Legion installed at York; the wooden fortress of Eboracum is built

71–4 Petilius Cerialis defeats the Brigantes

75 The palace at Fishbourne built

78–85 Agricola governor

80 London now houses a forum, basilica, governor's palace and even an amphitheatre

79–83 Agricola's campaigns in northern Britain and Caledonia

c.80 Eboracum fortress strengthened

84 The Romans do battle with the Caledonians at Mons Graupius, somewhere in modern day Aberdeenshire

90–6 Foundation of *colonia* at Lindum; Inchtuthil abandoned; Gleva fortress built

98–117 Trajan emperor; he orders a complete withdrawal from Scotland and the construction of a new frontier between Newcastle-on-Tyne and Carlisle

100 Many of the 8,000 miles of Roman roads in Britain are completed, allowing troops and goods to travel easily across the country

107–8 Eboracum fortress rebuilt in stone

117–38 Hadrian emperor

c.117 Roman defeat, heavy casualties

122 Hadrian in Britain

122–8 To strengthen the border between Roman-occupied Britain and Scotland, Hadrian orders the famous wall be built. Significantly, many of the early forts along Hadrian's Wall face south into the intractable Brigantes' territory, showing the ongoing threat they posed

c.122 VI Legion replaces IX Legion

125–30 Major fire in London

139–40 The Antonine Wall built, dramatically shifting the Rome's northern border. It is built of earth and timber, strengthened by a series of forts

155 St Albans, one of the largest towns in Roman Britain, is destroyed by fire

155–158 The Antonine Wall is abandoned and Roman troops withdraw back to Hadrian's Wall. The cause is unknown, however it may have been because of an uprising by the Brigantes or the Antonine smallpox plague

165–80 Antonine smallpox plague ravages the Roman army empire-wide

182 The Brigantes, along with tribes of southern Scotland and northern England, rise again against the Romans. Fighting continued for years along Hadrian's Wall, with towns further south building precautionary preventative defences

193–211 Septimius Severus emperor

193–7 Albinus, governor of Britain, attempts to become emperor, taking the army of Britain to the continent; Hadrian's Wall overrun

197 Destruction of York's fortress by the Maeatae: subsequent rebuilding; Hadrian's wall fortified

197 Severus defeats Albinus near Lyons

208–11 Severus in Britain: political and military administration reorganised. Caledonia invaded

211 Severus dies in York; the area between the two walls is now a protectorate – Britain is divided up into two separate provinces; the south called 'Britannia Superior' ('superior' indicating that it was closer to Rome), with the north called 'Britannia Inferior'. London was the new capital of the south, with York the capital of the north. The adjacent civil town becomes a *colonia*

211 Death of Severus at York

211–17 Marcus Antoninus emperor

250–71 Plague of Cyprian assails the Roman empire

250 onwards – new threats to Britannia emerge as the Picts from Scotland, as well as the Angles, Saxon and Jutes from Germany and Scandinavia

259 Britain, Gaul and Spain secede from the Roman Empire, creating the so-called 'Gallic Empire'

274 The Gallic Empire is re-absorbed into the main Roman Empire

284 Diocletian introduces the system of two Augusti and two Caesars

287 The admiral of the Roman Channel fleet, Carausius, declares himself Emperor of Britain and Northern Gaul, and starts minting his own coins

293 Carausius is assassinated by his treasurer, Allectus, who starts to build his palace in London to strengthen his claim to authority. He also builds the famous 'Saxon Shore Forts' along the coasts of Britain, both to strengthen defences against the Germanic tribes to the east but also to prevent Rome from sending a fleet to reclaim Britain for the empire

296 The Roman Empire retakes Britannia and Allectus is killed in battle near Silchester. Britain is then divided into four provinces; Maxima Caesariensis (northern England up to Hadrian's Wall), Britannia Prima (the south of England), Flavia Caesariensis (the Midlands and East Anglia) and Britannia Secunda (Wales)

293 Constantius I (Chlorus) Caesar of the West

296 Constantius Caesar defeats Allectus and retakes Britain. Northern tribes overrun northern half of Roman Britain. York and Chester destroyed and subsequently rebuilt

300 Hadrian's Wall increasingly dilapidated. Repaired and rebuilt. New military command – Dux Britanniarum – in charge of the field army. HQ in York

306 Constantius I defeats the Picts and invades Caledonia. Death of Constantius I at York. Constantine proclaimed emperor

313 Edict of Milan grants tolerance to Christian church

314 Christianity now legal in the Roman Empire, thanks to Constantine amongst others; Bishop of York at Council of Arles

343 Emperor Constans visits Britain

364–9 Major raids by Picts, Scots, Attacotti and Saxon pirates. Hadrian's Wall rebuilt

367–83 Gratian emperor

367–9 Combined raids by Saxons, Picts and Scots. Hadrian's Wall outflanked. Fullofaudes, Duke of Britain, routed. Count Theodosius in Britain – repairs wall

383–8 Usurpation by Magnus Maximus, commander in Britain, who conquers Gaul and Spain

388 Magnus Maximus defeated by Theodosia at Aquileia

395–423 Honorius emperor; Sertorius reorganises Britain; troops withdrawn

396 Massive barbarian attacks on Britain resume. Large naval engagements are ordered against the invaders, with reinforcements arriving from other parts of the empire

399 Peace is fully restored throughout Britannia

401 Many troops are withdrawn from Britain to assist with the war against the Goths led by Alaric I, who is intent on sacking Rome

407 The remaining Roman garrisons in Britain proclaim one of their generals, Constantine III, Emperor of the Western Roman Empire. Constantine quickly levies an army and crosses the English Channel to invade Gaul and Spain, leaving Britain with only a skeleton force to defend itself

410 With more and more incursions from the Saxons, Scots, Picts and Angles, Britain turns to the Roman emperor Honorius for help. He responds, telling them to 'look to their own defences' and refuses to send any aid. This effectively marks the end of Roman Britain

[Adapted in parts from 'Chronology of York and the Empire', in *An Inventory of the Historical Monuments in City of York, Volume 1, Eboracum, Roman York* (London, 1962), p. 44. British History Online http://www.british-history.ac.uk/rchme/york/vol1/p44 [accessed 19 December 2018].

Appendix 1: Select list of Roman emperors

Emperors from Augustus to Constantine

Emperor	Reign
Augustus (Imp. Caesar Augustus)	27 BC–AD 14
Tiberius (Ti. Caesar Augustus)	AD 14–37
Gaius / Caligula (C. Caesar Augustus Germanicus)	37–41
Claudius (Ti. Claudius Caesar Augustus Germanicus)	41–54
Nero (Imp. Nero Claudius Caesar Augustus Germanicus)	54–68
Galba (Ser. Sulpicius Galba Imp. Caesar Augustus)	68–69
Otho (Imp. M. Otho Caesar Augustus)	69
Vitellius (A. Vitellius Augustus Germanicus Imp.)	69
Vespasian (Imp. Caesar Vespasianus Augustus)	69–79
Titus (Imp. Titus Caesar Vespasianus Augustus)	79–81
Domitian (Imp. Caesar Domitianus Augustus)	81–96
Nerva (Imp. Caesar Nerva Augustus)	96–98
Trajan (Imp. Caesar Nerva Traianus Augustus)	98–117
Hadrian (Imp. Caesar Traianus Hadrianus Augustus)	117–138
Antoninus Pius (Imp. Caesar T. Aelius Hadrianus Antoninus Augustus Pius)	138–161
Marcus Aurelius (Imp. Caesar M. Aurelius Antoninus Augustus)	161–180
Lucius Verus (Imp. Caesar L. Aurelius Verus Augustus)	161–169
Commodus (Imp. Caesar M. Aurelius Commodus Antoninus Augustus)	176–192
Pertinax (Imp. Caesar P. Helvius Pertinax Augustus)	193
Didius Julianus (Imp. Caesar M. Didius Severus Julianus Augustus)	193
Septimius Severus (Imp. Caesar L. Septimius Severus Pertinax Augustus)	193–211
Clodius Albinus (Imp. Caesar D. Clodius Septimius Albinus Augustus)	193–197
Pescennius Niger (Imp. Caesar C. Pescennius Niger Justus Augustus)	193–194
Caracalla (Imp. Caesar M. Aurelius Antoninus Augustus)	198–217
Geta (Imp. Caesar P. Septimius Geta Augustus)	209–211

Macrinus (Imp. Caesar M. Opellius Macrinus Augustus)	217–218
Diadumenianus (Imp. Caesar M. Opellius Antoninus Diadumenianus Augustus)	218
Elagabal (Imp. Caesar M. Aurelius Antoninus Augustus)	218–222
Severus Alexander (Imp. Caesar M. Aurelius Severus Alexander Augustus)	222–235
Maximinus (Imp. Caesar C. Julius Verus Maximinus Augustus)	235–238
Gordian I (Imp. Caesar M. Antonius Gordianus Sempronianus Romanus Africanus Senior Augustus)	238
Gordian II (Imp. Caesar M. Antonius Gordianus Sempronianus Africanus Iunior Augustus)	238
Balbinus (Imp. Caesar D. Caelius Calvinus Balbinus Augustus)	238
Pupienus (Imp. Caesar M. Clodius Pupienus Augustus)	238
Gordian III (Imp. Caesar M. Antonius Gordianus Augustus)	238–244
Philip (Imp. Caesar M. Julius Philippus Augustus)	244–249
Decius (Imp. Caesar C. Messius Quintus Traianus Decius Augustus)	249–251
Trebonianus Gallus (Imp. Caesar C. Vibius Trebonianus Gallus Augustus)	251–253
Volusianus (Imp. Caesar C. Vibius Afinius Gallus Veldumnianus Volusianus Augustus)	251–253
Aemilianus (Imp. Caesar M. Aemilius Aemilianus Augustus)	253
Valerian (Imp. Caesar P. Licinius Valerianus Augustus)	253–260
Gallienus (Imp. Caesar P. Licinius Egnatius Gallienus Augustus)	253–268
Claudius II (Imp. Caesar M. Aurelius Claudius Augustus)	268–270
Quintillus (Imp. Caesar M. Aurelius Claudius Quintillus Augustus)	270
Aurelian (Imp. Caesar Domitius Aurelianus Augustus)	270–275
Tacitus (Imp. Caesar M. Claudius Tacitus Augustus)	275–276
Florianus (Imp. Caesar M. Annius Florianus Augustus)	276
Probus (Imp. Caesar M. Aurelius Probus Augustus)	276–282
Carus (Imp. Caesar M. Aurelius Carus Augustus)	282–283
Carinus (Imp. Caesar M. Aurelius Carinus Augustus)	283–285
Numerianus (Imp. Caesar M. Aurelius Numerius Numerianus Augustus)	283–284
Diocletian (Imp. Caesar C. Aurelius Valerius Diocletianus Augustus)	284–305
Maximian (Imp. Caesar M. Aurelius Valerius Maximianus Augustus)	286–305
Constantius (Imp. Caesar Flavius Valerius Constantius Augustus)	305–306
Galerius (Imp. Caesar C. Galerius Valerius Maximianus Augustus)	305–311
Severus (Flavius Valerius Severus Augustus)	306–307
Maxentius (M. Aurelius Valerius Maxentius Augustus)	306–312
Constantine (Imp. Caesar Flavius Valerius Constantinus Augustus)	307–337
Licinius (Imp. Caesar Valerius Licinianus Licinius Augustus)	308–324
Maximin (C. Valerius Galerius Maximinus Augustus)	308/9–313

Emperors from Diocletian to Romulus

Emperor West	Reign	Emperor East	Reign
Maximian	C. 285–286, A. 286–305, 307–310	Diocletian	A. 284-305
Constantius I	C. 293–305, A. 305–306	Galerius	C. 293-305, A. 305–311
Constantine	C. 306–308, A. 308–337	Maximin	C. 305-308, A. 308–313
Severus	A. 306–307		
Maxentius	A. 307–312	Licinius	A. 308–324
		Licinianus	C. 317–323
Crispus	C. 317–325	Martinianus	C. 324
		Constantine	A. 324–337
Constantine II	C. 317–337, A. 337–340	Constantius II	C. 324–337, A. 337–361
Constans	C. 333–337, A. 337–350		
Dalmatius	C. 335–337	Gallus	C. 350–354
Constantius II	A. 351–361		
Julian	C. 355–360, A. 360–363	Julian	A. 361–363
Jovian	A. 363–364	Jovian	A. 363–364
Valentinian I	A. 364–375	Valens	A. 364–378
Gratian	A. 375–383		
Maximus	A. 383–387	Theodosius I	A. 379–395
Valentinian II	A. 383–392		
Theodosius I	A. 394–395		
Honorius	A. 395–423	Arcadius	A. 395–408
Constantius III	A. 421	Theodosius II	A. 408–450
Valentinian III	A. 425–455	Marcian	A. 450–457
Petronius Maximus	A. 455		
Avitus	A. 455–456		
Majorian	A. 457–461	Leo I	A. 457–474
Libius Severus	A. 461–465		
Anthemius	A. 467–472		
Olybrius	A. 472		
Glycerius	A. 473		
Julius Nepos	A. 473–480	Leo II	A. 474
Romulus	A. 475–476	Zeno	A. 474–491
		Anastasius	A. 491–518
		Justin I	A. 518–527
		Justinian	A. 527–565
		Justin II	A. 565–578
		Tiberius Constantine	C. 574–578, A. 578–582
		Maurice	A. 582–602

Appendix 2: Governors of Britannia AD 43–97

Britannia was a consular province, so its governors had first to serve as a consul in Rome before they could be governor.

Claudian governors

    Aulus Plautius (43–47)
    Publius Ostorius Scapula (47–52)
    Aulus Didius Gallus (52–57)
    Quintus Veranius (57–57)
    Gaius Suetonius Paulinus (58–62)
    Publius Petronius Turpilianus (62–63)
    Marcus Trebellius Maximus (63–69)

Flavian governors

    Marcus Vettius Bolanus (69–71)
    Quintus Petillius Cerialis (71–74)
    Sextus Julius Frontinus (74–78), also a military writer
    Gnaeus Julius Agricola (78–84), conqueror of Caledonia
    Sallustius Lucullus (?; 84–c.89)
    Aulus Vicirius Proculus (*fl.*93)
    Publius Metilius Nepos (?; c.96–c.97)

Appendix 3: York's medieval churches built using Roman masonry

All Saints, North Street	1166	Active
St Andrew, Fishergate	Pre conquest	Demolished fourteenth century
St Andrew, St Andrewgate	1194	Converted use
St Cuthbert, Peasholme Green	Pre conquest	Converted use
St Helen on the Walls, Aldwark	Late ninth century	Demolished sixteenth century
St Mary Bishophill Jnr	Pre conquest	Active

York churches with a Roman connection

St Cuthbert, Peaseholme Green

York's oldest church after the Minster, close to Layerthorpe Postern on York city walls near Layerthorpe; the east wall of the chancel is built from Roman masonry and is situated at the north east corner of the fortress where excavations have shown large gaps in the fortress' perimeter wall. A tile bearing the stamped inscription LEG IX HISP has been found.

St Denys, Walmgate

There is evidence of previous Roman and Viking and Anglo-Saxon buildings on the site: a third-century Roman altar unearthed in 1846 from underneath a church pillar was dedicated to the Roman God Arciaco, erected by the Roman centurion Maternius Vitalis; it is now in the Yorkshire Museum. The inscription reads: *'To the god Arciaco and to the Divinity of the Emperor, Mat(…) Vitalis, centurion, willingly and deservedly fulfilled his vow'*.

St Helen, Stonegate
This church is dedicated to St Helen, mother of Constantine the Great. St Helen appears in the stained glass.

St Helen-on-the-Walls, Aldwark
This church was on or near the east corner of York's Roman walls; it was a small rectangular building, with stone walls that included re-used Roman stones and built in the late ninth or early tenth century. Camden would have us believe that the emperor Constantius I was buried here in AD 306; so far so good … Camden then adds that in the sixteenth century excavations revealed a vault in which a candle from 306 was still burning!

St Martin-cum-Gregory, Micklegate
The 1844 tower plinth is made from stone pillaged from the Roman temple of Mithras.

St Mary, Bishophill Senior
One of the tiles used as the base of a culvert discovered under St Mary Bishophill Junior by Peter Wenham bore the imprint of an animal's paw over the impression of a child's sandal which in turn showed the stitching on the sole.

St Mary, Bishophill Senior
St Mary has the unenviable distinction of being the last medieval church in York to be demolished. There were Roman walls underneath the church; pieces of Roman tilework can be seen in the tower. Excavations in the vicinity in the '60s revealed a ninth-century Anglian antler comb together with numerous oyster shells.

The remains of nearly 2,000 fish were collected in a compacted mass making it reasonable to conclude that something in the region of 40,000 fish were present within the excavated area, with many more unexcavated. The fish were small herrings (*Clupea herengus*) and sprats (*Clupea sprattus*) imported into York in the late Roman period. All were 4–6 inches long. They were dried and not smoked or salted, possibly rejected as being too small to bother with.

St Mary, Castlegate
The church is eleventh century, but most of what can be seen is fifteenth century; it boasts a dedication stone denoting the church a minster, and records that it was founded by [Ef]rard, Grim and Æse. A recycled Roman column capital and fragments of three column drums have been revealed under the chancel arch.

St Michael, Spurrriergate
St Michael was thought to be more than a match for the devil, so it is no surprise that many churches from the earliest times were dedicated to him on pagan sites. This church of St Michael stands on what was the site of the Roman temple of Hercules.

St Sampson, Church Street
St Sampson is the only church in the country dedicated to St Sampson. According to Geoffrey of Monmouth's *History of the Kings of Britain*, he was installed by King Arthur's uncle, Ambrosius Aurelianus, as Archbishop of York after repelling a force of Saxon invaders in AD 466. This Sampson, of course, has nothing to do with the Samson in the Bible – he of the long hair and Delilah. The church was built into the wall of the old Roman fortress.

York Minster
In the excavations under the central tower the remains of the earlier Norman church show it to be built of Roman ashlars, including a centurial stone.

Appendix 4: Roman legions serving in Britannia

Legio II *Augusta* – The Second Augustan Legion

Legio VI *Victrix* – The Sixth Victorious Legion

Legio VIII *Augusta* – The Eighth Augustan Legion

Legio IX *Hispana* – The Ninth Spanish Legion

Legio XIV *Gemina* – The Fourteenth Twin Legion

Legio XX *Valeria* – The Twentieth Legion, Valiant and Victorious

Legio XXII *Deiotariana* – The Twenty-Second Deiotarian Legion

Legio XXII *Primigenia* – The Twenty-Second Firstborn Legion

Some Latin terms

aedes	shrine
aedile	public officer responsible for public works, entertainment, and the distribution of grain, markets etc.
aerarium	the public treasury
ala	wing of an army; usually a contingent of allies, about the size of a legion
auxilia	troops provided by Rome's allies (*socii*)
castra	military camp
centuria	a unit of the Roman legion; of varying size, around 80–100.
centurio	commander of a century
civitas sine suffragio	citizenship without suffrage – a form of citizenship granted to towns (eg Capua in 338 BC) who were subject to Roman taxation and military service, but were denied the right to vote or hold political office
classis	fleet; also the Roman soldiers who made up the bulk of the armies. The *infra classem* were less wealthy, lightly-armed skirmishers
cognomen	a man's third name; a woman's second. The name of a legion
cohors	one of ten sub-units of a legion
colonia	then highest level of town populated with Romans; a settlement for army veterans
Comitia Centuriata	the assembly of citizens which legislated, elected magistrates, declared war, ratified treaties, and judged capital offences
consul	the highest political office on the *cursus honorum*; two elected annually (usually).

	Consuls held *imperium*
cursus honorum	the sequence of public offices held by men of senatorial class
damnatio memoriae	the erasing of records, statuary, and the memory of *persona non grata* after their death
decimation	the execution of every tenth man, chosen by lot from the ranks
dictator	temporary absolute leader, appointed for a limited period to resolve a crisis
dies nefasti	inauspicious days
dignitas	political dignity, related to tenure of offices in the *cursus honorum*
dilectus	the annual military levy
dona militaria	military decorations
dux	leader
equites	the equestrian order ranked below senators; the *equites* were middle class businessmen and farmers; cavalry
exercitus	army
fetialis	war priest responsible for ensuring that Rome's wars were just in the eyes of the gods. Responsible for the rites performed for declaring war and concluding peace
fides	trustworthiness, good faith, loyalty – a quality the Romans were anxious to be seen to uphold, including respect for the law and *fides* in foreign relations
foederati	nations to which Rome provided benefits in exchange for military assistance
foedus	originally a sacred oath made by a fetial priest on behalf of the Roman people; a treaty
gens	family; clan, e.g. Claudii
genius loci	spirit of the place
gladius	short sword
glans	slingshot
hasta	spear
hastati	soldiers of the second class, who stood in the

	front line; green, raw recruits
Hellenism	a culture of classical Greece, which percolated into Rome in the second century BCE
imperium	power, command, empire; power, particularly that power bestowed on consuls, generals, and praetors
indutia	cease-fire
laudatio	eulogy
legio	legion; a levy of troops
lex	law
magister equitum	second-in-command to the dictator; the master of the horse usually commanded the cavalry, as the dictator was forbidden to ride a horse
maiestas	power; authority; treason
manipulus	maniple; sub-unit of the legion, comprising two centuries
miles	soldier
mos maiorum	the way the ancestors did things or behaved
numen	divine power, spirit
opus signinum	concrete
patricius	patrician; the dominant political class; aristocratic families
pax	peace
phalanx	close-knit body of heavily-armed infantry
pietas	dutifulness – in all aspects of life
pilum	javelin
plebeian	non-patricians
porta decumana	the rear gate (in the garden at Gray's Court)
porta praetoria	under St Helen's Square
porta principalis dextra	gate at the right-hand end of the transverse street (under Bootham Bar)
porta principalis sinistra	gate at the left-hand end of the transverse street (under King's Square)
praefectus	prefect, commander of an auxiliary force
preafectus urbi	prefect of the city
praetor	public office, responsible for justice. Second-

	highest political and military office
Principate	the period of the emperors, from 27 BCE onwards
principes	troops in their twenties and thirties
proconsul	acting consul
Republic	the period of Republican government in 509–43 BCE
res gestae	political and military achievements
rex	king
scutum	shield
signifer	standard-bearer
socius (pl. *socii*)	ally
testudo	tortoise-shaped formation in which shields are interlocked above the head
triarii	veteran troops
tribuni plebei	officials responsible for protecting their fellow plebeians against injustices from the patricians; had a veto and sacrosanctity
tribunus militum	military tribune
triumphator	a general who had been awarded a triumph
triumphus	triumph: the military procession along the Via Sacra, in Rome, for victorious generals. Spoils of war, prisoners, and captured chieftains were paraded. The enemy chieftains were sometimes executed; the triumphator rode in a chariot, and was dressed as Jupiter
tumultus	crisis
vates	soothsayer; prophetess; priestess
velites	lightly-armed skirmishing troops. 1200 or so in a legion
via decumana	the rear street; in York, Chapter House Street
via praetoria	Stonegate
via principalis	main street – Petergate
virtus	manliness; courage; virtue

Further Reading

Addyman, P. V., 'Excavations in York, 1972–1973, First Interim Report', *Antiquaries Journal*, 54 (1975): 200–31

Addyman, P. V., *York: British Historic Towns Atlas*, volume V:5 (Historic Towns Trust: Oxford, 2015)

Allason-Jones, L., *Women in Roman Britain* (British Museum Press: London, 1989)

Allason-Jones, L., *Roman Jet in the Yorkshire Museum* (Yorkshire Museum: York, 1996)

Anderson, A. S., *Roman Military Tombstones* (Shire Publications: Aylesbury, 1984)

Bartie, A., L. Fleming, M. Freeman, T. Hulme, A. Hutton, P. Readman, '"The York Pageant", The Redress of the Past', http://www.historicalpageants.ac.uk/pageants/1354/

Bartie, A. *Restaging the Past: Historical Pageants, Culture and Society in Modern Britain* (UCL Press: London, 2019)

Bartie, A., 'Pageants and the Medieval Past in Twentieth-Century England', *English Historical Review*, 133 (2018): 866–902

Bartie, A., 'The Redress of the Past: Historical Pageants in Twentieth-Century England', *International Journal of Research on History Didactics, History Education and History Culture – Yearbook/Jahrbuch/Annales*, 37 (2016): 19–35

Bedoyere, G., *Roman Britain: A New History* (Thames and Hudson: London, 2010)

Bennett, J., *Towns in Roman Britain* (Shire Publications: Oxford, 2001)

Betts, I., (unpublished) 'A Scientific Investigation of the Brick and Tile Industry of York to the mid-eighteenth century', Ph.D. thesis (University of Bradford, 1985)

Bidwell, P., *The Roman Army in Northern England* (The Arbeia Society: Newcastle, 2009)

Birley, E. B., 'The Roman inscriptions of York', *Yorkshire Archaeological Journal*, 41 (1966): 726–34

Birley, E. B., 'The Fate of the Ninth Legion', in Butler, R. M., *Soldier and Civilian in Roman Yorkshire* (Leicester University Press, Leicester, 1971), 71–80

Bishop, M. C., *Handbook to Roman Legionary Fortresses* (Pen and Sword Military: Barnsley, 2013)

Bishop, M. C, *The Secret History of the Roman Roads of Britain* (Pen and Sword Military: Barnsley, 2014)

Boutwood, Y., 'Roman Fort and Vicus, Newton Kyme, North Yorkshire', *Britannia*, 27 (1996), 340–4

Branigan, K., *Roman Britain: Life in an Imperial Province* (Reader's Digest: London, 1980)

Branigan, K., *Rome and the Brigantes: the impact of Rome on northern England* (J. R. Collis Publications: Sheffield, 1980)

Breeze, D. J, 'Roman Military Deployment in North England', *Britannia*, 16 (1985): 1–19

Breeze, D. J., *Roman Forts in Britain* (Shire Archaeology: Oxford, 2002)

Breeze, D. J., *The Frontiers of Imperial Rome* (Pen and Sword Military: Barnsley, 2011)

Brinklow, D., 'Coney Street, Aldwark and Clementhorpe, Minor Sites and Roman Roads', *The Archaeology of York* 6/1 (1986)

Brinklow, D., 'Fortress wall in bus lay-by', *Interim: Archaeology of York* 12 (1987), 16–18

Brittany, T., 'Imperial Statues and Public Spaces in Late Antiquity: Conceptualising "Constantine" at York as an Ancient Public Commission', in Mandichs (ed.) 2016, *Proceedings of the Twenty-Fifth Annual Theoretical Roman Archaeology Conference* (Theoretical Roman Archaeology Conference: Leicester, 2015), 177–87

Broadhead, W., 'Colonization, Land Distribution, and Veteran Settlement', in *A Companion to the Roman Army*, ed. P. Erdkamp (Blackwell: Oxford, 2007), 148–63

Buckland, P. C., 'The Environmental Evidence from the Church Street Roman Sewer System', *Archaeology of York* 14/1 (London: Council for British Archaeology, for the York Archaeological Trust, 1976) 1976.

Burn, A. R., *Agricola and Roman Britain* (English Universities Press: London, 1953)

Burn, A. R., *The Romans in Britain – An Anthology of Inscriptions* (Blackwell: Oxford, 1969)

Burnham, B. C., *The Small Towns of Roman Britain* (Batsford: London, 1990)

Butler, R. M. (ed.), *Soldier and Civilian in Roman Yorkshire* (Leicester University Press: Leicester, 1971)

Butler, R. M., 'The Defences of the Fourth Century Fortress at York', in Butler, *Soldier and Civilian in Roman Yorkshire* (Leicester University Press: Leicester, 1971), 97–106

Campbell, D.B., *Roman Auxiliary Forts 27BC–AD378* (Osprey Publishing: Oxford, 2009)

Charlesworth, D., 'The Defences of *Isurium Brigantum*', in Butler, *Soldier and Civilian in Roman Yorkshire* (Leicester University Press: Leicester, 1971), 155–64

Chrystal. P., *Roman Military Disasters* (Pen and Sword Military: Barnsley, 2016)

Chrystal, P., *How to Be a Roman* (Amberley Publishing: Stroud, 2017)

Chrystal. P., *When in Rome: A Social History of Rome* (Fonthill Media: Stroud, 2017)

Chrystal, P., *Women at War in the Ancient World* (Pen and Sword Military: Barnsley, 2017)

Chrystal, P., *Roman Records and Communication* (Fonthill Media: Stroud, 2018)

Chrystal. P., *Reportage from Ancient Greece & Rome* (Fonthill Media: Stroud, 2019)

Chrystal, P., 'Death', in *Oxford Bibliographies in Classics* ed. Ruth Scodel (Oxford University Press: New York, 2020)

Chrystal, P., *The Romans in the North of England* (Destinworld Publishing: Darlington, 2019)

Chrystal, P., *A Historical Guide to Roman York* (Pen and Sword Books: Barnsley, 2021)

Collingwood, R. G., *The Archaeology of Roman Britain* (Methuen and Co.: London, 1930)

Collingwood, R. G., *The Roman Inscriptions of Britain [RIB]* (Clarenden Press: Oxford, 1965)

Cool, H. E. M., 'Glass-making and the Sixth Legion at York', *Britannia*, 30 (1999): 147–62

Cool, H. E. M., 'Craft and industry in Roman York', in P. Wilson (ed.), *Aspects of Industry in Roman York and the North* (Oxbow Books: Oxford, 2002), 1–11

Cool, H. E. M., 'Which "Romans"; what "home"? The myth of the "end" of Roman Britain', in Haarer, F. K. (ed.), *AD 410: The History and Archaeology of Late and Post-Roman Britain* (Society for the Promotion of Roman Studies: London, 2014)

Cool, H. E. M., *Finds from the Fortress*, Archaeology of York 17/10 (Council for British Archaeology: York, 1995)

Cox, M., 'Ageing adults from the skeleton', *Human Osteology in Archaeology and Forensic Science* (Cambridge University Press, 2000)

Dean, W.T. 'Yorkshire jet and its links to Pliny the Elder', *Proceedings of the Yorkshire Geological Society*, 56 (2007): 261–5

de la Bedoyere, G., *The Finds of Roman Britain* (Batsford: London, 1989)

Dickinson, B. M. 'The Evidence of Potters' Stamps on Samian Ware and on Mortarie for the Trading Connections of York' in Butler, *Soldier and Civilian in Roman Yorkshire* (Leicester University Press: Leicester, 1971), 127–42

Dobinson, C., *Aldborough Roman Town* (English Herigage: London, 1995)

Downes, A., *50 Finds from Yorkshire: Objects from the Portable Antiquities Scheme* (Amberley Publishing: Stroud, 2016)

Dyer, J., 'Excavations and discoveries in a cellar in Messrs. Chas. Hart's premises, Feasegate, York, 1956', *Yorkshire Archaeological Journal*, 39 (1967): 419–25

Eckardt, Hella et al., 'A Lady of York: migration, ethnicity and identity in Roman Britain', *Antiquity* (March 2010)

Evans, D. T., 'Excavations at the former Daveygate Centre', *Interim: the Archaeology of York*, 22.4 (1998): 5–9

Evans, D. T., 'The former Primitive Methodist chapel, 3 Little Stonegate', *Interim: the Archaeology of York*, 23.2 (2000): 24–8

Frere, S., *Britannia: A History of Roman Britain*, revised edition (Routledge & Kegan Paul: London, 1978)

Garlick, T., *Roman Sites in Yorkshire* (Dalesman Publishing: Clapham, 1971)

Gillespie, C. C., *Boudica: Warrior Woman of Roman Britain* (Oxford University Press: Oxford, 2018)

Hall, R. A., 'Excavations in the Praetentura: 9 Blake Street', *Archaeology of York*, AY3/4 (1997)

Hall, R. A., 'Roman warehouses and other riverside structures in Coney Street', in D. Brinklow, *Coney Street, Aldwark and Clementhorpe, Minor Sites and Roman Roads* 6/2 (Archaeology of York: York, 1986)

Hall, R. A., 2004. 'The topography of Anglo-Scandinavian York', in R. A. Hall et al. (eds), *Aspects of Anglo-Scandinavian York* 8/4 (Archaeology of York: York, 2004), 488–97

Hanson, W. S., *Agricola and the Conquest of the North* (Batsford: London, 1991)

Hartley, B. R., 'Roman York and the Northern Military Command to the Third Century AD', in Butler, *Soldier and Civilian in Roman Yorkshire* (Leicester University Press: Leicester, 1971), 55–70

Hartley, B. R., *The Brigantes* (Sutton Publishing: Stroud, 1988)

Hartley, E., *Roman Life at the Yorkshire Museum* (Yorkshire Museum: York, 1985)

Hartley, E. (ed.), *Constantine the Great: York's Roman Emperor* (Lund Humphries: London, 2006)

Higham, N. J., *The Carvetii* (Sutton Publishing: Stroud, 1985)

Highways England, *A1 Leeming to Barton improvement scheme: Archaeological discoveries* (Highways England: Guildford, 2018)

Holst, M., *The Headless Gladiators of York*, Ancient Mysteries Series, 19/05/2017 (Channel 5: London, 2017)

Hunter Mann, K., 'The Starting Gate Tadcaster Road, Dringhouses, York', *York Archaeological Trust Evaluation Report* 9 (1996)

Hunter Mann, K., 'Romans lose their heads in York', *York Historian* 23 (2006): 2–7

Ireland, S., *Roman Britain: A Sourcebook*, 3rd ed. (Routledge: London, 2009)

Jaques, D., 'Vertebrate Remains from Excavations at the Minster Library, York', *Reports from the Environmental Archaeology Unit, York* 99/39 (1999)

Jarrett, M. G., 'Non-legionary troops in Roman Britain: Part One, The Units' *Britannia*, XXV (1994): 35–77

Johnson, P., *Romano-British Mosaics* (Shire Publications: Princes Risborough, 1995)

Jones, C., *York: Archaeological Walking Guides* (The History Press: Stroud, 2012)

Jones, R. H., *Roman Camps in Britain* (Amberley Publishing: Stroud, 2012)

Kenny, J., 'Investigating the Roman road from Eboracum towards Aldborough, near Hessay and Moor Monkton', *York Historian*, 30 (2013): 43–5

Kenward, H. K., 'Environmental Evidence from a Roman Well and Anglian Pits in the Legionary Fortress' *Archaeology of York* 14/5 (1986)

Leach, S., 'A Lady of York: migration, ethnicity and identity in Roman Britain', *Antiquity*, 84 (2010): 131–45

Lewis, M. J. T, *Temples in Roman Britain* (Cambridge University Press: Cambridge, 1966)

Ling, R., *Romano-British Wall Painting* (Shire Publications: Princes Risborough, 1985)

Ling. R., 'Brading, Brantingham and York: a new look at some fourth-century mosaics', *Britannia*, 22 (1991)

Lister, M., 'Some Observations upon the Ruins of a Roman Wall and Multangular-Tower at York', *Philosophical Transactions of the Royal Society*, 13 (1683): 238–42.

Liversidge, J., *Britain in the Roman Empire* (Cardinal Books: London, 1973)

Liversidge, J., 'Brantingham Roman Villa: discoveries in 1962', *Britannia*, 4 (1973)

Livingstone, H., *In the Footsteps of Caesar: Walking Roman Roads* (Dial House: Shepperton, 1995)

MacGregor, A., 'Finds from a Roman Sewer and an Adjacent Building in Church Street', *Archaeology of York*, 17/1 (1976)

Macnab, N., 'More on the Roman fortress: a lift-pit excavation behind 3 Little Stonegate', *Interim: the Archaeology of York*, 23(3) (2000): 31–46

Mainman, A., 'Craft and economy in Anglo-Scandinavian York', in R. A. Hall et al. (eds), *Aspects of Anglo-Scandinavian York*, Archaeology of York 8/4 (Council for British Archaeology: York, 2004), 459–87

Mann, J. C., *The Romans in the North* (Durham, 1975)

Mann, J. C., 'The Creation of Four Provinces in Britain by Diocletian', *Britannia* 29 (1998): 339–41

Margary, I. D., *Roman Roads in Britain: Volume II North of the Foss Way – Bristol Channel* (London Phoenix House: London, 1957)

Margary I. D., *Roman Roads in Britain* (third edition) (London, 1973)

McComish, Jane, 'The Former Starting Gate PH, Dringhouses, York', York Archaeological Trust Web Report, Report Number AYW8 (2004)

Miller, S., 'Roman York: excavations of 1925', *Journal of Roman Studies* 15 (1925): 176–94

Miller, S., 'Roman York: excavations of 1926–1927', *Journal of Roman Studies*, 18 (1928): 61–99.

Millett, M., *The Romanization of Britain: An Essay in Archaeological Interpretation* (Cambridge University Press: Cambridge, 1990)

Millet, M. (ed.), *Shiptonthorpe, East Yorkshire: Archaeological Studies of a Romano-British Roadside Settlement* (Yorkshire Archaeological Society: Leeds, 2006)

Milsted, I., 'The Roman Landscape of Blossom Street', *York Historian* 27 (2010)

Monaghan, J. 1993: Roman Pottery from the Fortress: 9 Blake Street, Archaeology of York 16/7, York

Monaghan, J., 'Roman Pottery From York', *Archaeology of York* 16/8 (Council for British Archaeology: York, 1997)

Moore A., 'Hearth and Home: The Burial of Infants within Romano-British Domestic Contexts', *Childhood in the Past*, 2:1 (2009): 33–54

Moorhead, S., *The Romans Who Shaped Britain* (Thames and Hudson: London, 2012)

Neal. D. S., *Roman Mosaics of Britain: Volume I: Northern Britain* (Illuminata Publishers for The Society of Antiquaries of London: London, 2002)

Norman, A. F., *The Romans in East Yorkshire* (East Yorkshire Local History Society: Hull, 1960)

Norman, A. F. *Religion in Roman York*, in Butler, *Soldier and Civilian in Roman Yorkshire* (Leicester University Press: Leicester, 1971), 143–54

Ordnance Survey, *Roman Britain; Historical map and guide* (Ordnance Survey: Southampton, 1994)

Ottaway, P., '7–9 Aldwark', *Interim: the Archaeology of York* 10 (1985): 13–15

Ottaway, P., *A Traveller's Guide to Roman Britain* (Historical Times: London, 1987)

Ottaway, P., 'The Roman fortress: planning for the future', *Interim: the Archaeology of York* 16(3) (1991): 3–13

Ottaway, P., *The English Heritage Book of Roman York* (Batsford: London, 1992)

Ottaway, P., 'Excavations and Observations on the Defences and Adjacent Sites, 1971–90', *The Archaeology of York* 3/3 (York Archaeological Trust and Council for British Archaeology: York, 1996)

Ottaway, P., 'The sewer trenches in Low Lane, Petergate', *Interim: the Archaeology of York* 22(3) (1997): 15–23

Ottaway, P., *Roman York* (Tempus: Stroud, 2004)

Ottaway, P., *Roman Yorkshire: People, Culture and Landscape* (Blackthorn Press: Pickering, 2013)

Pearson, N. F., 'The Purey Cust Nuffield Hospital', *Interim: the Archaeology of York* 11 (1986): 15–18

Pearson, N. F., 'Swinegate excavation', *Interim: the Archaeology of York* 15(1) (1990): 2–10

Percival, J., *The Roman Villa – An Historical Introduction* (Batsford: London, 1976)

Phillips, A. D. and Heywood, B. *Excavations at York Minster, vol. I: Roman to Norman, The Headquarters of the Roman Legionary Fortress at York and Its Exploitation in the Early Middle Ages (71–1070 AD)* (HMSO: London, 1995)

Philpott, R. A., *Burial Practices in Roman Britain* (Oxford: British Archaeological Reports: Oxford, 1991)

Price, J., 'Broken Bottles and Quartz-Sand: Glass Production in Yorkshire and the North in the Roman Period',.in P. R. Wilson (ed.), *Aspects of Industry in Roman Yorkshire and the North* (Oxbow Books: Oxford, 2002), 81–93

Radley, J., 'A section of the Roman fortress wall at Barclay's Bank, St Helen's Square, York', *Yorkshire Archaeological Journal* (1966): 41, 581–4

Radley, J., 'Two interval towers and new sections of the fortress wall, York', *Yorkshire Archaeological Journal* (1970): 42, 399–402

Radley, J., 'Excavations on the defences of the city of York in an early medieval stone tower and the successive earth ramparts', *Yorkshire Archaeological Journal* (1972): 44, 38–64

Raistrick, A., *The Romans in Yorkshire* (Dalesman Publishing: Clapham, 1972)

Ramm, H. G., 'Roman York: excavations of 1955', *JRS* (1956): 46, 76–90

Ramm, H. G., 'The End of Roman York', in Butler, *Soldier and Civilian in Roman Yorkshire* (Leicester University Press: Leicester, 1971), 179–200

RCHM (Royal Commission on Historical Monuments), *Roman Camps in England – The Field Archaeology* (HMSO: London 1995)

RCHME (Royal Commission on Historical Monuments England), *An Inventory of the Historical Monuments in the City of York*, vol. 1: Eboracum, Roman York (HMSO: London, 1962)

RCHME (Royal Commission on Historical Monuments England), *An Inventory of the Historical Monuments in the City of York* vol. 5: The Central Area (HMSO: London, 1981)

Richmond, I. A., 'The British Section of the Ravenna Cosmography', *Archaeologia* vol. 93 (1949): 1–50

Rivet, A. L. F., *Town and Country in Roman Britain* (Hutchinson: London, 1964)

Rivet, A. L. F., *The Place-Names of Roman Britain* (Batsford: London, 1979)

Rollason. D. W., *Sources for York History to AD 1100* (York Archaeological Trust: York, 1998)

Roskams, S., Neal, C., Richardson, J. and Leary, R., 'A Late Roman Well at Heslington East, York: ritual or routine practices?', *Internet Archaeology* 34 (2013)

Rowland, T. H., *The Romans in North Britain* (F. Graham: Newcastle, 1970)

Rowland, T. H., *Roman Transport in the North of England* (F. Graham: Newcastle, 1976)

Salway, P., *Roman Britain* (Oxford University Press: Oxford, 1985)

Shotter, D. C. A., *The Roman Frontier in Britain* (Carnegie Publishing: Preston, 1996)

Shotter, D. C. A., 'Cerialis, Agricola and the Conquest of Northern Britain', *Contrebis* XXIV (1999)

Shotter, D. C. A., *Roman Coins from North-West England: second supplement* (Centre for North-West Regional Studies: Lancaster, 2000)

Sitch, B., *Roman Humberside* 2nd edn. (Humberside County Council Archaeology Unit: Hull, 1992)

Smith, D. J., *The Roman Mosaics from Rudston, Brantingham and Horkstow* (City of Kingston upon Hull Museums and Art Galleries: Hull, 1976)

Smith, D. J., *Roman Mosaics at Hull*, third edition (Hull City Museums & Art Galleries: Hull, 2005)

Smith, R. A., 'The Roman Pavement from Horkstow', *The British Museum Quarterly* vol. 2, no. 2 (1927): 44–6

Southern, P., 'Signals versus Illumination on Roman Frontiers', *Britannia* 21 (1990): 233–42

Spratt, D. A., 'Prehistoric and Roman Archaeology of North-East Yorkshire', *CBA Research Report* 87 (1990)

Stead, I. M., 'Excavations at the south corner of the Roman fortress at York, 1956', *Yorkshire Archaeological Journal* 39 (1958): 515–38

Stead, I. M., 'An excavation at King's Square, York, 1957', *Yorkshire Archaeological Journal* 42 (1968): 151–64

Stead, I. M., 'Yorkshire Before the Romans: Some Recent Discoveries', in Butler, *Soldier and Civilian in Roman Yorkshire* (Leicester University Press: Leicester, 1971), 21–44

Stiles Johnson, M., 'Excavations of a Roman camp at Huntington South Moor, York', *York Historian* 29 (2012)

Stockwell, M., 'Sorry about the smell but ...', *Interim: the Archaeology of York* 15(1) (1990): 20–5

Summerton, N., *Medicine and Health Care in Roman Britain* (Shire Publications: Aylesbury, 2007)

Swan, V. G., 'Legio VI and its men: African legionaries in Britain', *Journal of Roman Pottery Studies* 5 (1992): 1–33

Swan, V. G., 'A Rhineland potter at the legionary fortress of York', in M. Aldhouse-Green, *Artefacts and Archaeology. Aspects of the Celtic and Roman World* (University of Wales Press: Cardiff, 2002), 190–234

Taylor, J., 'An Atlas of Roman Rural Settlement in England', *CBA Report* 151 (2007)

Terry, J. E. H., *The Book of the York Pageant 1909* (Ben Johnson and Co.: York, 1909)

Tilley, E., *Old Collections, New Questions: Researching the Roman Collections of the Yorkshire Museum* (Yorkshire Museum: York, 2018)

Tillott, P. M. (ed.), *A History of the County of York: The City of York* (Victoria County History: London, 1961)

Todd, M., 1973, *The Coritani* (Duckworth: London, 1973)

Todd, M., 'The Claudian Conquest and its Consequences', in Todd, M., *A Companion to Roman Britain* (Blackwell: Oxford, 2004), 57

Wacher, J. S., 'Yorkshire Towns in the Fourth Century', in Butler, *Soldier and Civilian in Roman Yorkshire* (Leicester University Press: Leicester, 1971), 165–78

Wacher, J., *The Towns of Roman Britain* (Batsford: London, 1974)

Webster, G. A., *The Roman Conquest of Britain* (Batsford: London, 1965)

Webster, G. A., 'A Hoard of Roman Military Equipment from Fremington Hagg', in Butler, *Soldier and Civilian in Roman Yorkshire* (Leicester University Press: Leicester, 1971), 107–26

Wenham, L. P., 'Excavations and discoveries adjoining the south-west wall of the Roman legionary fortress in Feasgate, York, 1955–57', *Yorkshire Archaeological Journal* 40 (1961): 329–50

Wenham, L. P., 'Roman and Viking Discoveries in York' *Illustrated London News* (May 26, 1962)

Wenham, L. P., 'Excavations and discoveries within the legionary fortress in Davygate, York, 1955–58', *Yorkshire Archaeological Journal* 40 (1962): 507–87

Wenham, L. P., 'Discoveries in King's Square, York, 1963', *Yorkshire Archaeological Journal* 42 (1968): 165–8

Wenham, L. P., 'The Beginnings of Roman York' in Butler, *Soldier and Civilian in Roman Yorkshire* (Leicester University Press: Leicester, 1971), 45–54

Wenham, L. P., 'Excavations in Low Petergate, York, 1957–8', *Yorkshire Archaeological Journal* 44 (1972): 65–113

Wenham, L. P., *Eboracum* (Ginn and Co.: London, 1978)

Whitwell, J. B., *The Church Street Sewer and an Adjacent Building*, Archaeology of York 3/1 (Council for British Archaeology: York, 1976)

Wilson, P., *Aspects of Industry in Roman Yorkshire and the North* (Oxbow Books: Oxford, 2003)

Wilmott, T., *The Roman amphitheatre in Britain* (Tempus: Stroud, 2008)

Wilmott, T. (ed.), 'Roman amphitheatres and spectacula; a 21st-century perspective. Papers from an international conference held at Chester, 16th–18th February 2007', *British Archaeological Reports* (Archaeopress: Oxford, 2009)

Witts, P., *Mosaics in Roman Britain* (Tempus: Stroud, 2005)

Wood, I., 'Turning a fortress into a cathedral', *British Archaeology* 7 (1995): 7

Woods, A., 'Constantine the Great and the Wold Newton Hoard' – lecture given at the York Architectural and York Archaeological Society Meeting (The Yorkshire Archaeological and Historical Society: Leeds, October 17, 2018)

Wright, R. P., 'Tile stamps of the sixth legion found in Britain', *Britannia* 7 (1976): 224–35

Wright, R. P., 'Tile stamps of the ninth legion found in Britain', *Britannia* 9 (1978): 379–82

Websites

www.paulchrystal.com

https://www.cam.ac.uk/research/news/road-radar-to-reveal-yorks-roman-secrets

http://www.british-history.ac.uk/rchme/york/vol1/pp5-47 British History Online

www.digforeboracum.co.uk/ York's forthcoming Roman Quarter attraction

https://digyork.com/ DIG is a hands-on archaeological adventure giving kids the chance to become trainee 'diggers' and discover the most exciting artefacts from 2000 years of York's history! Tours last one hour

https://romaninscriptionsofbritain.org/ 'Hosts Volume One of The Roman Inscriptions of Britain, R.G. Collingwood's and R.P. Wright's magisterial edition of 2,401 monumental inscriptions from Britain found prior to 1955. It also incorporates all Addenda and Corrigenda published in the 1995 reprint of *RIB* (edited by R.S.O. Tomlin) and the annual survey of inscriptions published in Britannia since'.

https://en.wikipedia.org/wiki/Roman_sites_in_Great_Britain by modern county

https://en.wikipedia.org/wiki/List_of_Roman_place_names_in_Britain

https://en.wikipedia.org/wiki/List_of_Latin_place_names_in_Britain

https://www.google.com/maps/d/viewer?ll=53.60099751285261%2C-1.0509274027702986&z=7&mid=1m055UlJWsufwKQwGAxMR6iI5-6M Roman sites in Britain

https://en.wikipedia.org/wiki/ Roman_roads_in_Britannia

http://www.romanroads.org/rrragazetteer/rr72b/rr72b.html

https://web.archive.org/web/20061231090447/http://www.roman-britain.org/tribes/brigantes.htm

https://finds.org.uk/ Portable Antiquities Scheme database run by the British Museum and National Museum Wales to encourage the recording of archaeological objects found by members of the public in England and Wales. So far the Scheme's network have recorded over 1 million objects, all of which are accessible via the PAS database.

http://www.yorkosteoarch.co.uk/ York Osteoarchaeology

http://thesebonesofmine.wordpress.com/category/york-osteoarchaeology/
https://www.yorkarchaeology.co.uk York Archaeological Trust
http://vindolanda.csad.ox.ac.uk/exhibition/history-3_to.shtml Vindolanda tablets on line
http://www.northofthetyne.co.uk/HWC1.html Hadrian's Wall east to west
https://www.pastscape.org.uk/
http://www.romanroads.org/historicalbackground.html – Roman Roads Research Association
https://www.british-history.ac.uk/rchme/york/vol1/ – an inventory of Roman monuments in York and the access roads to the city
www.paulchrystal.com
www.yayas.org.uk Yorkshire Architectural & York Archaeological Society
A. Bartie, P. Caton, L. Fleming, M. Freeman, T. Hulme, A. Hutton, and P. Readman, The Redress of the Past: Historical Pageants in Britain, 1905–2016 (database, published online, 2016, at http://www.historicalpageants.ac.uk/pageants/)

Some recent books by Paul Chrystal:

A History of Britain in 100 Objects (2022)
A History of the World in 100 Pandemics, Epidemics & Plagues (2021)
How to be a Roman: A Life in the Day of a Roman Family (2017)
War in Greek Myth (2020)
The Romans in the North of England (2019)
A Historical Guide to Roman York (2021)
For a full list see www.paulchrystal.com

Other Yorkshire Architectural & York Archaeological Society publications

The Bars and Walls of York – A Handbook for Visitors, R. M. Butler
Medieval York, R. M. Butler
Photographs and Photographers of York, the Early Years, 1844–1879, Hugh Murray
York Historian – journal of the Yorkshire Architectural & York Archaeological Society

INDEX

*Pages in italics indicate an illustration

Aesculapius, 19, *19*
Agricola, Gnaeus Julius, 30, 56, *57*, 68, 84, 166
Agriculture, 89–90
Allectus, 36, 183
Altars, 71ff, 146–7
Amphitheatre, Roman, 52–3
Antonine Itinerary, 60
Arimanius, 75, 147–8, *148*
Atrocities, 92ff, 99ff, 107–8
Atys, 75
Augustus, 38–9, 81–3, 86, 99

Barracks, 41, 43, 107
Basilica, 41, 69
Bath, Roman, 20–1, *21*, 61ff
Baths, public, 47, 48, 71–2
Bishop Eborius of Eboracum, 37
Boudica, 30, 56, 83, 166
Brigantes, 29, 30, 57, 68, 84
Burials, 87, 92ff, *95*, *98*, 144–6, *144–6*

Caer Caradoc, Battle of, 83
Caledonian Confederacy, 35
Canaba, 2, 87ff
Calgacus, 31, 167
Caracalla, 35, 58, 75–6, *132*
Cemeteries, see Burials
Chariots, 25, *25*
Child murder, 107–8
Christianity, 37–8, 144
Clades Lolliana, 39
Claudius, 39–40
colonia, 2, 29, 36, 44, 56ff, 59, 67, 75, 76f, 82, 87
Commodus, 86
Constantine the Great, 2, 3, 25, 26, 36, *36*, 37, *37*, 59, *60*, 66, 75, 108, 114, 136, *137*, 170, 171

Constantius Chlorus, 11, 36
Construction, 58, 79, *178–9*
Contubernium, 82
Cornu, cornum, 22, *22*
Cursus publicus, 81

Dio Cassius, 35
Diocletian, 36, 75, 183
Diocletian Reforms, 36
Domitian, 32, 172
Druids, 31

Eboracum (Drake, 1788), 72, 98–9
Eboracum or York Under the Romans (Wellbeloved 1842), 72
Eboracum Annual Roman Festival, 164, 165
Eboracum 1900th Anniversary, 1971, 168, *168*
Esher, Lord, 42
'First Hour of the Crucifixion', 5, *5*
Food, 89–90
Foreign policy, Roman, 32, 33, 39–40, 68
Four Seasons Mosaic, 140–3, *140–3*
Funerals, 89–91

Gaius Suetonius Paulinus, 56
Genocide, 35
Gladiators, 99ff, *102–4*, 134
'Grave of a Rich Lady', 144–6, *144–6*

Hadrian, 75, 84, 86
Haxby Hoard, 171, *171*
Heslington Hoard, 172, *172*
Historia Augusta, 75
Hoards, 169–72
Hunting, 89

Industry, 87–9, 109ff

Jet, 109–14, *110, 112, 113, 144, 145*
Julia Velva, 89–91, *90*
Julius Frontinus, 29, 30

lares, 135, *135*
Legio II *Adiutrix*, 56
Legio II *Augusta*, 30
Legio II *Parthica*, 35
Legio VI, 58, *58*, 85–6, *85*
Legio IX, *Hispana*, 30, 56, 58, 66, 67, 76, 83–4, *84*, 93, 99, 122, *122*, 125
Legio XX, *Valeria Vitrix*, 56, 68
Legion, *legio*, 82–3
Legionaries, 86–7

Maeatae, 35
macellum, 71
mansiones, 55, 70, 81
Marcus Aurelius, 152, 173–4, *173*
Mars, 14, *1, 12, 134*, 149–50
Martial, 63–4
Military installations, 30, 31–2, 33, 35
Mineral resources in Britannia, 30, 39, 58
Mithras, 75
Mons Graupius, Battle of 31, 33, 68, 167
Mosaics, 38, 55, 64, 76, 88, *13*, 140–3, *140–3*
Municipium, 87

Nero, 86

Ophiotaurus, 139, *139*
Ordovices, 31
Osteoarchaeology, 99ff, 107–8, *136*, 144–6, *144–6*
Overton Hoard, 172
Ovid, 139

Parasites, intestinal, 54–5
Parisi, 29, 30, 57, 68
Picts, 30, 36
Plaques, 25
Pliny the Elder, 99, 110
Ptolemy, 60, 168

Quintus Petillius Cerealis, 29, 30, 65, 83, 181

Ravenna Cosmography, 60
Religion, 3, 72–5, 92, 146
Rivers, 81
Road Radar 2022 Project, 176–7, *177*
Roads, 77ff, *78*
Roman column, 6, *6*, 25, 26, 69–70, *69*, 119
Roman Quarter, vii, 178–9, *178*
Romanisation, 30, 31, 78, 167
Royal Commission on Historical Monuments for England (RCHME), 41, 42
Ryedale Hoard, 173, *173*

Sanitation, 54–5, 70–1
Scots, 30, 36
Selgovae, 31, 32, 166
Seneca the Younger, 62–3
Septimius Severus, 35, 57, 58, 66, 73, 75, 93, 114, 118, 168, 172
Serapis, 72–5, *74*, 123
Severan Reforms, 35
Sewer, Roman, 23, *24*, 54–5
Signal stations, 36
Silures, 30
Social life, 87

Tacitus, 29, 30, 38, 56, 166
Teutoburger Wald, Battle of, 39, 40, 83
Trade, 88, 109ff
Trajan, 57, 122, 152, 181
Troop numbers, 33, 77, 86

Venutius, 29, 83
Vespasian, 56, 181
Vettius Bolanus, 65
via principalis, 9, 26, 68, 81
vicus, 38, 51, 67, 76, 87ff, 89, 186
Vindolanda tablets, 60, 86

Walls, Roman, 7, *7, 12*, 14, 17, *18*, 19, *20*, 42, 48
Wells, Roman, 11, *11*, 50, 54
Wenham, Peter, 41, 51–2, 183
Wold Newton Hoard, 169, *170*
York Archaeological Trust (YAT), 42ff, *43*

Index of Places

*Pages in italics indicate an illustration
** Places in bold are in York

Aldborough, 36
Aldwark, 55, 76, 109, 138, 183
Aldwark Tower, 7, 26
Ampleforth, 173
Anglian Tower, 16, *16*, 42
Antonine Wall, 33, *34*, 35, 36, 86
Anglesey, 31
Aquae Sulis, see Bath

Bath, 63, *64*
Blake Street, 43–4, 107, 171
Blossom Street, 51
Bootham, 71
Bootham Bar, 8, *9*, 9, 10, *10*, 25, 26, 68
Bridlington, 30, 89
Britannia, 30 and *passim*
Britannia Inferior, 35, 56, 59, 76
Britannia Secunda, 36, 59
Britannia Superior, 35
Britannic Empire, 36
Brough-on-Humber, 30, 57, 71, 79

Cade's Road, 79
Caerleon, 30, 35, 53, 81
Caledonia, 32, 35, 84, 166
Calcaria, see Tadcaster
Camulodunum, see Colchester
Castleshaw, 30
Cawthorne, 30, 78
Chester, 35, 52–3, *53*, 81
Clementhorpe, 88
Colchester, 56
Coney Street, 76, 81

Davygate, 20, 41, 57, 61, 66
Dere Street, 32, 79

Derventio, see Malton
Deva, see Chester
DIG York, 162, *163*
Diocese of the Britons, 36
Dolaucothi, 30
Driffield Terrace cemetery, 48, 99ff, 102–4
Dringhouses, 88–9

(East) Heslington, 50–1, 89, 172
Eboracum, 29, 35 and *passim*
Eburacum, 60
Ermine Street, 79

Foss, River, 88

Goathland, 30, 78
Goodramgate, 7, 24, 122

Hadrian's Wall, 33, 35, 47, 59, *59*, 68, 75, 84, 85, 86
Hardknott (*Mediobogdum*), 34
Haxby, 171, *171*
High Ousegate, 23
High Petergate, *9*, 68
Housesteads, 59
Hungate, 48, 49, *49*
Huntington, 51

Ilkley, 30
Inchtuthil, 33, 68
Isca Augusta, *see* Caerleon
Isurium Brigantum see Aldborough
Judges' Lodgings, 19

Gask Ridge, 33

King's Manor possible amphitheatre, 52–3

Lendal, 19
Lincoln, 56, 57, 71, 79, 81, 83, 88
Lindum, see Lincoln

Malton, 30, 57, 79, 150
Micklegate, 71–2
Micklegate-Skeldergate-Queen's Hotel, 48
Monk Bar, 7, 8, 26
Mount, The, 95
Multangular Tower, 13–14, *13*, *14*, 15, *15*, 16, 42, 48, 59, *60*, 65, 93, 152
Museum Gardens, 13, 164, *165*

Nessgate, 23, 87
Newington Hotel, 51–2, 99

Ouse, River, 87, 88

Petergate, see High Petergate
porta decumana, 8, 27, 68
porta praetoria, 27, 68
porta principalis dextra, 10, 11, *11*, 27, 68
porta pricipalis sinistra, 24, 27, 68
principia, 3, 6, 27, 41, 36, 66, 69, 81, 114, 115, *115*, *116–17*
Petuaria, see Brough-on-Humber
Praetorian Gate, *19*
Prefecture of Gaul, 36
Pumsaint, 30

Railway station site, 47
Robin Hood Tower, 8, 26
Roman Bath Museum, 20, *20*, 21, 160–1, *160–1*

Rougier Street, 44
Ryedale, 173

Saltburn, 30
Scarborough, 30
Slack, 30
Stamford Bridge, 89
Stanwick, 29, 57
St Helen's Square, 19
St Leonard's Hospital, 17, *18*, 48
Stonegate (*via praetoria*), 25, 25, 36, 68
St Sampson's Square, 20–1, *20*
St Stephen's Chapel, 5, *5*

Tadcaster, 58, 70
Tanner Row, 45
Theatre Royal, York, 11
Treasurer's House, 24
Toft Green, 72–4
Trentholme Drive Roman cemetery, 41, 93ff, *101*

Undercroft Museum, 3, 4, 114ff, *115–19*

via decumana, 24, 27
via praetoria, 25, 26
via principalis, , 26
Vindolanda, 60, 107

Wade's Causeway, 78
Wellington Row, 44–5, 46
Whitby, 109–14

York, 29 and *passim*
York Minster, 2, 3, *3*, 41, 65, 114ff
Yorkshire Museum, 16, *17*, 120ff